URBAN EDUCATION:
THE CITY AS A LIVING CURRICULUM

Claude Mayberry, Jr.
Editor

ASCD

The Association for Supervision and Curriculum Development
225 North Washington Street · Alexandria, VA 22314

Editing:
Ronald S. Brandt, ASCD Executive Editor
Nancy Modrak, Assistant Editor
Nancy Olson, Senior Editor

Cover Design:
Amy Rupp

Stock Number: 611-80206
Library of Congress Catalog Card Number: 80-67288
ISBN 0-87120-100-3

Contents

This book is dedicated to my loving aunt, Rose L. Harwell.

CLAUDE MAYBERRY, JR.

ACKNOWLEDGMENTS

I wish to express my deep appreciation to the people who made this book pos-
sible, the contributing authors, and the following people who took time to write
and share their professional opinions about educational problems in urban areas:
Gordon McAndrew, Roscoe C. Brown, Jr., Dorothy T. Bryant, Lawrence A.
Cremin, Carrie B. Dawson, Sidney H. Estes, Nicholas Hobbs, Stephen Horn,
George Hutt, Michael P. Marcase, A. Harry Passow, Glenn E. Porter, Otha L.
Porter, Rabbi Murray Saltzman, George A. Schlekat, Rebecca Segal, and
William W. Turnbull. I would also like to express my appreciation to the mem-
bers of the ASCD Working Group on Black Concerns, where the idea for the
book originated.

Finally, I wish to extend my appreciation and thanks to Barbara Zinn for
her editorial assistance and to Susan Evangelist for her clerical assistance.

CLAUDE MAYBERRY, JR.

Foreword

Consider this startling statement from Mayberry's introduction: "Educationally deprived urban adults will be re-educated not at all, and their children will be re-educated only partially." If we accept the validity of this statement, then we have reason to fear for the future of our nation— for it is questionable whether the pressures and tensions spawned in our urban settings can simmer for two generations without a volcanic explosion.

As the authors point out so dramatically and eloquently, our schools in general are in trouble. For whatever reasons, and we can argue interminably about the justness or unjustness of the criticism, public confidence in American education is at a low ebb. Nowhere in education is the criticism more pointed or more vocal than in our urban schools. Here the problems that afflict schools have coalesced into a malignancy. Here are the decaying buildings and the hopeless parents. Here are the truly deprived.

If this book makes one point, it is that we must begin to treat the illness of our urban schools. We may start by admitting that these conditions exist. It is all too convenient to pretend that problems in urban education are distorted or, worse, that they are the result of some inherent deficiency among the people they serve who need not be consulted about the schools their children attend.

Mayberry's statement continues: "But for their grandchildren there is hope that re-education will not be warranted." The chapter on "Urban Educational Leadership" cites examples of schools that are working despite the handicaps shared by urban schools in general. In one case, we see the effect of a caring faculty who arrives early, stays late, and has high expectations of the students. In another case, we learn that urban schools do not have to accept low academic standards as a fact of life. And we see that dynamic educational leadership can exist in the disadvantaged urban setting.

There is much here for study, debate, and reasoned discussion. The authors have put together a disturbing book, a book that should cause each of us to look more closely at our own attitudes toward education—particularly education in the most challenging environment in America today, the inner core of our major cities.

BARBARA D. DAY
President, ASCD, 1980-81

Preface

At the center of our nation are cities, our havens of commerce, culture, and the majority of our people. At the center of our cities are educational institutions which foster our nation's most valuable resources—our children and, therefore, our future. No issue or concern is of a higher priority than the proper and effective education of our children. This concern transcends government–imposed boundaries, whether urban, suburban, or rural. Urban education, however, is of special concern to Americans, for it encompasses the entire spectrum and multiplicity of interests and concerns which best characterize our nation.

Our cities are in crisis because of unemployment, poverty, shrinking tax bases, crime, alienation, and a declining sense of community. The crisis of the city invariably affects the quality of its educational system, for that system usually is a reflection of the surrounding community. The crises of both urban education and cities in general must be resolved if our nation is to survive and prosper.

The first step in resolving any crisis is to understand and appreciate that crisis. Claude Mayberry, Jr., and other distinguished educators have made a significant step toward this understanding and appreciation in *Urban Education: The City as a Living Curriculum*. Mayberry has brought together five comprehensive studies on the most critical areas facing urban schools today. Each deals with a separate problem area and its historical development. Solution-oriented techniques are clearly articulated by the authors. The primary emphasis is one that has endured since the advent of progressive education—a school concept that calls for the involvement of the total community. Community involvement within the educational process is central to resolving the urban educational crisis. Not only must the community become involved in the educational process, but the community interests, diversity, culture, and prospects must be reflected in the curriculum, instruction, and administrative decision-making process.

vii

What issues or problems should become the focus of urban educational reform? Certainly the attitudes and behavior of all participants; the quality and commitment of leadership both internal and external to educational institutions; curriculum, both in relationship to content and context; and proper finance which reflects both adequacy and equity are all important foci. These issues and the application of solutions tailored to the urban environment are discussed. The authors place special emphasis on addressing the needs of all citizens and place responsibility for educational quality on the community as a whole.

The first area discussed is "Attitudes and Behavior." Authors Mayberry, Crossley, and Sweet describe the sociological and psychological factors that keep the urban poor from overcoming their powerless position. Disruptive behavior on the part of the urban poor, which is often misinterpreted, causes those in power to further disassociate; thus the situation in the inner city remains the same or further disintegrates. Solutions require total community involvement and accountability. The school administration working with the PTA could serve as a catalyst for bringing together institutions, families, churches, businesses, industries, and other agencies in the private and public sectors to implement social programs of common interest and benefit to the total community. Understanding the diversity of the urban experience and its relationship to the nature of the school itself is crucial to designing and implementing a community-based educational system.

In the section entitled "Urban Educational Leadership," London addresses the question of whether an American education is meant for all the people. Schools derive their legitimacy from the production of a literate citizenry and there is a growing recognition that the schools are not doing this as well as they should. London states that the public looks to its schools to solve some social problems when ". . . a more reasonable function of public schools would be to make it possible for all children, regardless of background and scholastic aptitude, to acquire adequate skills in reading, writing, and practical arithmetic." Such a function, however, represents a real threat to the existing structure, which maintains the present system. The required change must come from dynamic leadership which demands that the schools educate all the children and respect, care for, and discipline them. Educational leaders must establish broader community involvement to find resolutions for varying views and differing values and philosophies. Successful implementation depends on a concerned faculty, who go beyond narrow pedagogical prescriptions, supported by students and parents.

Education must be designed to reflect the needs and aspirations of the people and communities it serves. Education should not reflect the class interest of only a few but should seek to provide self-respect and motivation for all who enter the school. The community in general cannot be expected to participate in or to support the school if it cannot identify how the school benefits the community. If the school serves only the interests of a narrow group, then the base of support and involvement will be just as narrow.

The task of building a new foundation for urban education requires changes in the relationship between the school and the community. Among the changes to be addressed are *the direction and purposes of education, effective community coalitions,* and *the reinvestment of faith in public or collective community enterprises.*

Education cannot be exclusionary, particularly in an urban environment. We must review carefully the history of education and understand how education has emerged relative to the interests of particular groups as opposed to all within the community. We must continue to rebuild educational systems based on the needs and interests of the entire community. Education should not seek to maintain the dominance of one group over another, but should be structured to create basic conditions where the interest of all is protected and all individuals are developed to their full potential.

In order to create community coalitions capable of changing and revitalizing urban education, we must have leadership from the traditional educational community as well as from the different communities to be served. If those in the community who have minimal power are provided with the professional support they need to make competitive yet reasonable input, then the patterns of rather elitist control of the schools will not simply continue under the guise of a new type of representative participation. It is not in the interest of any segment of the community to suppress or deny the maximum achievement of any other segment of the community. As London states in Chapter Two, "Public schools cannot continue to miseducate segments of their citizenry without ensuring the nation's demise in the long run." To the extent that the above principle guides in creating new community-based coalitions, we should have the basis for renewed faith in public or collective community enterprises.

We must be concerned with the declining interest and faith of our citizens in public organizations, and particularly the public schools which provide the basis for true harmony among our citizens.

The diversity of urban centers can only be reconciled through learning together, working together, and preparing for the future together. The public school aids in that process and provides a basis for future cooperation. Recently, many have decided to flee public schools by isolating themselves behind the protective walls of private institutions even when the cost has been extreme. This has only served to make a bad situation worse and in the long run will weaken the bonds that hold our society together. The best educational system will emerge when the overwhelming majority of children from all socioeconomic classes and all cultural backgrounds are educated together, for in the end they must live together.

MARION BARRY
Mayor, Washington, D.C.

Introduction
Claude Mayberry, Jr.

Educationally deprived urban adults will be re-educated not at all, and their children will be re-educated only partially. But for their grandchildren there is hope that re-education will not be warranted.

Public education is a right having priority over any privilege. The right to learn, however, has been thwarted in this country, particularly in urban areas, by a multitude of social and political obstacles. These obstacles are the many problems and crises which urban school districts face as they struggle to offer students an opportunity to learn. The inability to find viable solutions to these problems has further disadvantaged the urban community. For the past decade educational psychologists and sociologists have defined and redefined urban problems. Yet urban schools are still being strangled with a magnitude of barriers. National and state reading and mathematics achievement test data continue to provide evidence that those least affected by classroom "education" are those white and minority children of the lower socioeconomic classes. It is generally known that performance lags are most acute among certain ethnic groups—Native American, Hispanic and black children. These lags have a cumulative effect: those who are one year behind in the first grade are two years behind by the fourth grade, and by the sixth grade many are three years behind.

Who is to blame? Parents charge that administrators are far from educational leaders. Administrators charge that teachers are out of step with the concepts needed for a rapidly changing society. Administrators and teachers blame students for bringing their ethnicity and "cultural disadvantages" to the classroom, thus creating a situation with which they cannot cope. Administrators, teachers and students all charge that parents are disinterested, uninvolved, and educationally unqualified to deal with today's curriculum.

1

School administrators have not suffered from a paucity of proposed solutions to the dilemma of their failure to educate urban youth. There were educational advocates of the 1960's and 1970's who proclaimed that we should return to objective-based education, which focuses on outcomes rather than on processes and attitudes. Others advocated differentiation and tracking, believing that some students are genetically inferior, with brains too small to achieve. They opposed compensatory education. Then there are the Maslows, the behaviorists, and the environmentalists who advocate removing the social ills that inhibit the education of disadvantaged people, and who propose meeting survival needs first. Yet, when a solution is offered for a problem in one urban area, it is often declared useless in another. Many times what has been accepted as a solution in one school is not accepted in another school within the same district.

After two hundred years of self-government and a century of free, compulsory education, we still live in a nation that has more than forty million social dysfunctionals. These people do not understand simple forms of mathematics; they are unable to compose a descriptive paragraph or literate business letter and are helpless when required to fill out a social security application. They are unable to follow an instruction manual or balance a checking account. Eighty percent of the students entering high school in large urban districts have reading and arithmetic levels equivalent to those of the fourth or fifth grade.

Education is a $100 billion-a-year industry. Yet after urban children have been exposed to twelve years of the costliest education in the nation's history, we still ask why they cannot read, have no marketable skills, and have little or no preparation for work. Tenth-grade economics teachers were once astonished by the number of students entering their classes who could neither read nor compute above the fourth- or fifth-grade level. Today these same teachers (those who have not moved to suburban schools) expect this poor performance. They realize that it is ineffectual to attempt to educate their students in the techniques of establishing a company, of buying and selling stocks, of marketing a product or of advertising when over 70 percent of these students score below the 45th percentile on the national achievement tests in English and mathematics.

Children are being exposed to the terrors of the city behind the walls of schools once regarded as centers of learning. Today these institutions are centers of violence, drugs, corruption and terror, rapes and homicides. Parents who moved to the suburbs to escape from inner-city school problems find themselves back at the edge of the educational abyss they thought they had fled: drugs, vandalism, and declining achievement scores.

Many parents are beginning to view schools as dominated by unions whose interests lie in protecting and helping teachers instead of students.

There is an emerging awareness among parents that their children are being used as social pawns; they feel that public-school management has been taken over by political bureaucracy.

The 1960's and early 1970's were a period of experimentation and innovation in urban schools. Open classrooms became commonplace in elementary schools. New mathematics came to be the accepted approach to mathematics, although teachers were never trained to teach it. Today every school is unique, doing its "own thing." Every teacher is unique, doing his or her "own thing." We have achieved the right to be different at the expense of self-respect, respect for others, moral standards, and self-discipline.

The latest trend in resolving our literacy problem has been a back-to-basics movement. In large urban areas, tens of millions of dollars are spent each year for back-to-basics programs. Nevertheless, national testing services indicate that little progress in reading and math achievement has resulted from this increased spending. Why? Because we expect under-trained teachers and administrators to improve their curriculum and teaching just because their resources have been increased. Purchasing more teaching resources will not improve teaching and curriculum processes unless teachers are properly trained to use them.

Admittedly, there is a growing disillusionment with education, considering the millions of dollars which have been expended for highly touted programs that have not discernibly improved the quality of education or the aptitudes of students. As Edmund Burke once observed in a letter to a lord of Parliament, "To innovate is not to reform." In terms of education, his point is well taken. We have added layers of federal and state programs without appreciably changing the basic structure of American education. We are, however, emerging from an era of turmoil in education as we begin to distinguish between innovation and reform. We have learned from recent experience and have begun to fashion new ways to put that knowledge into practice.

Our experience over the last two decades has confirmed two important assumptions that are basic to American education. The first is that our instructional thrust should be based on the empirical assumption that most children, regardless of background, can learn basic skills to sustain them throughout life and make personal fulfillment possible; but we must realize that motivation and interest are the most significant contributions to such learning. The second assumption is that there is no standard which makes one educational pursuit more worthy than another. John Gardner observed, "The society which scorns excellence in plumbing because plumbing is a humble activity, and tolerates shoddiness in philosophy because philosophy is an exalted activity, will have neither good plumbing nor good philosophy. Neither its pipes nor its theories will hold water."

Interest in the special problems of public schools has been intense throughout the history of American education. This interest has been evinced in our pragmatic approach to areas of social concern in a continuing effort to modify and improve conditions. While the standard public school system may still be acceptable to many, we are now confronting a critical mass of discontented individuals for whom the public schools are no longer acceptable. Acceptability is affected by the complex status of these schools as well as by other persistent social problems.

It is impossible to describe in a single volume the status and complexity of the problems of public schools. It is a complexity which profoundly challenges efforts to change the meaning, function and scope of these schools, in relation to the transitional nature of the times. Having recognized these complexities, this author conducted a survey. Two hundred urban educators (superintendents, school board members, teachers, supervisors, junior and senior college faculty members and administrators, members of the Office of Education and of the Civil Rights Commission) were asked to identify what they believed to be the five most critical areas facing urban schools today. The most frequently mentioned areas were attitudes and behavior, educational leadership, curriculum, finance, and the politics of education.

Urban Education: The City as a Living Curriculum describes these specific problem areas and offers solution-oriented techniques that can be applied by any urban school community. This text is divided into six chapters: Attitudes and Behavior, Urban Educational Leadership, Developing Curriculum in an Urban Center, Financing for Primary and Secondary Education in the Urban Areas, Politics and the Curriculum, and Techniques and Recommendations for Change. Each of the authors believes that the community should be involved in the school curriculum; that anything short of total involvement denies the urban child an opportunity to develop to his full potential; and that the greater the separation between community and school, the less able the student will be to achieve and advance in his or her own environment.

Attitudes and Behavior

Mayberry, Crossley, and Sweet discuss, within the context of the urban community, the sociological and physiological interrelationships between the attitudes and behaviors of those who form the urban community, and how they relate to and affect inequity in educational resources and curriculum, integration and desegregation. Descriptive processes and techniques for changing adverse attitudes and behavior are outlined. The changes described in this chapter could ultimately pave the way for curricular modification that will have a positive impact upon the educational growth and development of all people in a particular urban community.

Urban Educational Leadership

This chapter does not presume to resolve the prevailing problems of public education. It does, however, treat some pertinent issues. Clement London examines the current situation of public schools in relation to their basic functions; he recommends change through leadership and suggests the mobilization of current available resources, given the conservative national mood and current fiscal exigencies.

These assertions indicate that no understanding and certainly no resolution of educational problems are possible without the collaborative efforts of students, parents, educators, institutional leaders, and, most importantly, classroom teachers, whose function it is to put the educational plan to use.

Developing Curriculum in an Urban Context

Curriculum is a highly significant component of urban education. It must consist of a plan for the education of pupils during their enrollment in a given school. This framework should be used by teachers, administrators, and supervisors as a point of departure from which to develop teaching strategies and requires the understanding and participation of the total community.

There are many unanswered questions pertaining to curriculum. For example, what is a viable content for urban curriculum plans? What are the basic skills necessary for urban growth and development? How does one develop curriculum plans to include these skills? What pedagogical techniques have been tested and proved to be most effective in the urban school setting? What is an effective, alternative testing program for urban schools, and how should this program be implemented through the curriculum plan?

The first section of this chapter discusses these questions and examines the failure of urban school personnel to accommodate themselves to the needs of urban youth. The second section focuses on other problematic questions: What kind of curriculum design could effectively encompass these goals and objectives and, at the same time, provide a frame of reference from which meaningful learning experiences could be derived? What processes would facilitate this type of urban curricular development?

Responding to these questions, authors Baptiste and Anderson describe models that have been or are being successfully used in some urban school districts. Finally, a six-step process is proposed to assist urban educators in utilizing the city as a living curriculum in their quest to develop learning models for their students.

Financing for Primary and Secondary Education in Urban Areas

Fiscal allocations to schools on the basis of local property values make the quality of a child's education a function of the school district's wealth, and thus constitute a violation of the Equal Protection Clause of the Fourteenth Amendment. Accordingly, educational finance systems at all levels of government are being challenged.

The loss of economic strength of our urban communities is attributable to the migration of upper- and middle-class families to the suburbs; the rise of minority and/or low-income populations; the shift of industrial and commercial businesses from cities to suburban regions; the increased demand for police and fire protection; and the rising cost of welfare, child care, family planning, and other social services. These changes have not only caused a depression in the tax base of urban communities, but have also resulted in reduced local funds for education. The suburban community, by nature, has minimal financial needs for social services; therefore more local funds and state categorical-aid grants can be channeled into educational resources.

Dick Netzer opens his book, *Economics of Property Tax,* by stating: "The American property tax abounds in anomalies. During the past century, no major fiscal institution, here or abroad, has been criticized at such length and with such vigor; yet no major fiscal institution has changed so little in modern times."

This chapter is a continuation of Netzer's criticism and attempts to engender change. More specifically, it focuses upon the regressive nature of the property tax, particularly the inordinate burden that it produces on the low-income urban household. Circuit-breaker techniques for easing these burdens are analyzed, and suggestions are made for legislative enactment of these techniques. The authors, Mark Gellerson and Claude Mayberry, recommend techniques for the development of alternative plans for improving the systems of financing urban education.

Politics and the Curriculum

Although it is a human right to learn, grow, and develop, it is not a fully legal right. The judicial system has effected numerous changes for equal opportunity to learn, but the system has done little to use the legal process in order to encourage enactment of legislation that would guarantee equal access to educational resources.

In the first part of this chapter, Mayberry reviews some of the legislation related to curriculum, finances of public schools, religion, and integration. He then describes how the political process operates at the local level to control the educational process. He examines how the school board, school administrators, teachers and parents politically influence the education of urban youth.

Techniques and Recommendations for Change

Chapter Six offers techniques and specific recommendations on how to use the political process to increase opportunities and equal access to a quality education for the urban school child. Mayberry raises some earnest questions: Do the privileges of professional and educational unions, school boards, school and government officials, and parents have priority over the right to educational growth and development of the urban child? Should the judicial system encourage greater federal intervention in urban educational crises? Should teachers and administrators be required to pass a national examination before being granted licenses to teach? Should licensed teachers and school officials be required to pass an examination periodically in order to retain their licenses? Should a school district be declared a disaster area if 25 percent or more of its teaching staff cannot comply with such criteria? Should legal and medical content be curricularized into the K-12 urban school curriculum?

Finally, Mayberry proposes an urban institute as a technique to utilize the total urban community as a living curriculum to foster the maximum growth of the urban child.

1

Attitudes and Behavior
Claude Mayberry, Jr., Mattie R. Crossley, and William H. Sweet

A Historical Perspective

The urban setting historically has been a conglomeration of diversified cultural practices, as groups of different ethnic backgrounds migrated to the cities seeking improvement in their lifestyles. Individuals tended to seek housing and employment near others of similar backgrounds. Consequently, the cultural practices of these individuals provided the nucleus for the development of smaller communities within larger communities. According to Clinard, "A major characteristic of urbanism is the diversity of interests and backgrounds of persons who at the same time live in close contact with one another." [1] The people living in urban communities vary in age, race, ethnic background, occupation, and in their interests, attitudes and values. Thus it follows that the first urban enclaves were spawned from the need for familiar faces, habits, and cultural ties.

Within each ethnic group, unofficial "laws" were established to set standards for those living within its boundaries. Inhabitants quickly learned the mechanisms for survival. They adopted what Rainwater terms "coping" skills or strategies for survival—the expressive lifestyle, the violent strategy, the strategy of depressive adoption, and the strategy of mobility.[2] In order to achieve acceptance, city dwellers approved certain behavior patterns and adopted them as a means to attain personal and community recognition. Nevertheless, behavior accepted in one enclave may have been frowned upon in another. Some individuals, upon learning the laws and following the social mores of their initial enclave, learned those of another enclave, changed their names when necessary, and moved with ease from one

[1] M. B. Clinard, *Sociology of Deviant Behavior,* 4th ed. (New York: Holt, Rinehart and Winston, 1974), p. 51.
[2] Ibid., p. 73.

9

enclave to another. Others, handicapped by color or language, could not readily enjoy this acclimation.

As classes developed, the affluent, the middle class, and the poor became more easily identified by the communities in which they lived, the jobs they held, the languages they spoke, and the mores they practiced. Subsequently, attitudes formed by city inhabitants varied according to the classes they represented.

Patterns of Behavior

Within any given urban setting, there are separate segments with varying achievements, interests, power bases, norms and values. While there are suburbs and areas within a city which exhibit economic stability, progress, and affluence, there are also areas within the city known primarily as "the slums" but now often referred to as the "metro core," or "blighted" area; and during the last decade, the term "ghetto" has become synonymous with Black and Hispanic slum areas. The people who reside in these areas are the ones who are denied or deprived of the quality of life enjoyed by the middle class and the affluent. Generally, these inhabitants know little about the power structure and its processes, have few economic resources, and exist in a "situation of poverty." [3] Therefore, the impoverished are affected by the value systems of others as much as by their own.

Traditionally, indigent families have been transient because of a lack of money to pay for essentials, such as rent. When the rent is due, these families simply find another place to live. Sometimes the small children in the family are sent to other family members for temporary keeping. If the living conditions do not improve, these children permanently remain in the households of other relatives for their upbringing. This type of behavior forces the lower economic groups into isolation from the larger community, where there is a greater degree of economic achievement and control over one's life.

Suffering benign neglect from the power structure, such families find that their influence is practically nonexistent. Their substandard housing conditions are ever-present; private industry is free to keep its job ranks closed to them; and merchants with whom they trade establish and maintain their own price guidelines without interference. Ostensibly, families in situational poverty must devise their own means of acquiring humane treatment.

[3] Gerald Leslie, Richard Larsen, and Benjamin Gordon, *Introductory Sociology: Order and Change* (New York: University Press, 1973), p. 388.

In the traditional urban community, as communication barriers develop between the affluent and the poor, feelings of suspicion, doubt, and distrust cause each group to become more deeply entrenched in their attitudes and behavior. Uninformed individuals not only develop personal prejudices, but perpetuate these debilitating nuances by covert and, often, overt means. Each succeeding generation, limited in its access to the mainstream, musters less hope of ever becoming an integral part of the proverbial "melting pot." The power structure makes little effort to change the conditions of the poor, but continues its own upward stride. Consequently, isolation of the poor is complete. Each class learns from the other via the media or by rumor. Thus, the affluent are regarded as leader-determiners by both the middle class and the poor.[4]

Psychological Patterns of Behavior

Because the poor perceive that the wealth and power of the affluent determine the course of politics, the highs and lows of economics, and the ins and outs of society and education, they lose much of their hope. Many feel that it is useless to strive for a better life. Anyone who takes more than a glance at both communities sees obvious differences. The streets of the affluent are swept and well lit; the streets of the poor are narrow, dusty and dark. The homes of the affluent are equipped with recreational luxuries, while the shacks of the poor quite often lack the essentials of water, toilet facilities, and adequate lighting. In the protected suburbs live the leader-determiners; in the projects live the poor and the hopeless. Leader-determiners are shielded from the poor by their affluence; the poor remain invisible.

The schools of the affluent are located amid spacious lawns; the buildings are dignified in appearance; the inside facilities suggest convenience and elegance. Public schools have been left to the poor, while private schools boast of ever-increasing enrollments of the affluent. Funding for public schools dwindles as more and more middle-class and upper-class parents send their children to private schools and, subsequently, lend their support to these schools.

Ill-equipped schools offer the children of the poor inadequate training; dwellings located near railroad tracks or in the midst of industrial complexes expose children to smog-filled air; and industrial sites where the poor

---

[4] Leader-determiners are those individuals who, because of their wealth, power, or influence, can affect courses of events and determine the destiny of others who are less wealthy, less powerful, and less influential.

work endanger their health and expose them to physical hazards and pesti-lence. As a result, it becomes economically and socially impossible for the affluent and the poor to live, work, or play together. Under these conditions, isolation evolves into acute alienation.

The general power structure looks upon slum dwellers as being inferior; in turn, slum dwellers reflect in their behavior their own suspicions of the "outside world." [5] These suspicions become generalized to include government, politicians, welfare groups, and the middle and upper classes.[6] Such suspicions evolve into prejudices and eventually become stereotypes, thus making the holders more susceptible to manipulation by the power structure. Unfortunately, the poor are further divided by race in a scramble for jobs, equal access to apprenticeships, and integrated education. The resultant economic and educational hardships suffered by the losers further separate them from the winners and prevent them from attaining equal opportunities in other areas.

Evidence indicates that deprivation induces children to adopt fatalistic attitudes, thus increasing the probability that they will fail to meet even their most basic needs.[7] Consequently, in the traditional urban community, fatalistic attitudes continue to prevail because the circumstances under which the attitudes were adopted remain unchanged.

Prevailing Perceptions

Societal patterns, particularly those based on color and race, wreak havoc on the creativity, self-image and personal aspirations of individuals in those groups suffering from deprivation. Many minorities living in the inner city feel there is virtually no hope for personal growth or economic betterment. Indications of failure among the poor are the high pathology rates (mental illness, unemployment, broken homes, suicide) which continue to plague them.[8]

To cope in a realistic sense, minorities rate possible opportunities for rewards and success and develop behavior mechanisms protective of their self-image; hence, many avoid confrontation with insuperable difficulties or failure. Their pervasive efforts to do what appears necessary, possible, and satisfactory under perceived circumstances affect the concepts they have of themselves.[9] The reputation of an individual in the slums as being trust-

---

[5] Clinard, pp. 61-62.
[6] Ibid., p. 72.
[7] Elinor F. McCloskey, ed., *Urban Disadvantaged Pupils, A Synthesis of 99 Research Reports* (Portland, Ore.: Northwest Regional Laboratory, 1967), p. 24.
[8] Leslie and others, p. 379.
[9] McCloskey, p. 24.

worthy might far outweigh middle-class consideration of the person as a criminal.[10] However, it should be noted that the merit of each perspective is determined by the respective group's value system—the group's definition of "trustworthiness" and "criminality"—which may not, on the one hand, recognize similarities between government welfare to families and government subsidies to big businesses, but, on the other hand, may readily assert the differences between capitalism and socialism. Thus, what appears to be necessary to the urban-minority-poor may seem insignificant to the urban economic and political leaders and to the leader-determiners.

In her synthesis of research reports on disadvantaged urban children, McCloskey highlights the following conclusions: self-effacement begins early in the lives of most black children; they inculcate early in life the notion that beauty, success, and status all wear a white skin; they acquire an awareness of stigma; some experience ego-deflation and a loss of self-esteem when they resist identification with their own racial group. Others, upon identifying with their parents, experience severely crippled self-images, low levels of expectancy, and little orientation toward school or the society it represents.[11] Conditioning designed to make not only the minority-poor but all minorities feel and act inferior is a daily occurrence. Subtly, often unconsciously, public officials, abetted by the media, convey the message that straight hair is somehow better than curly hair, that events in ethnic neighborhoods are less newsworthy and less important than events occurring elsewhere. Separate-but-equal schools are supported and knowledge of massive unemployment is disclaimed. Confronted by discontent within the minority-urban-poor community, political and economic leaders ask "What do *they* want?" "Why can't *they* pull themselves up?"

Young minority-poor observe the lack of opportunity among their ranks for high school or college graduates to become employed. The "success" of the neighborhood hustler is observed and envied. Parents and neighbors follow a here-and-now existence. The high school or college diploma has little effect on a future without prospects. The rationale that one must use one's energies to "outwit" the enemy, to accumulate symbols of wealth (big cars, flashy clothes, elaborate and ostentatious lifestyles) by whatever means possible, seems plausible. For the sake of sanity, the deviant behavior becomes the expected, normal behavior.

Little contact with the "outside" or predominately white world is to be expected. Physical isolation is encouraged. Anyone living outside the immediate community is viewed with intense suspicion. Feelings of aliena-

---

[10] Clinard, p. 71.
[11] McCloskey, pp. 25-26.

tion pervade the community and often erupt into displays of hostility toward the establishment and, frequently, within one's family and among one's peers. The school is tolerated until the compulsory attendance age is passed; what is taught in the schools has less value in helping one to "survive" than what is learned on the streets.

Conflicts in Modern Times

The value of an education is still being questioned by the young urban-minority-poor. Although the attitudes of parents, teachers, students and other community members may differ markedly, the outcome shows that deprived minority children who live in an urban environment cannot read, write, or count as well as middle-class minority or other middle-class or affluent children. The question of ultimate responsibility rests with the parents. Unfortunately, the parents of inner-city children generally lack educational achievement, which makes it difficult, if not impossible, for them to communicate to their children the benefits to be derived from education.[12] An additional problem of separating the ideal from the real further complicates the task, since both parents and children are aware of many instances in which education seems to have little or no bearing on the quality of one's life. Consequently, these conflicts create confusion regarding the purposes and values of education.

Moreover, economically poor parents are aware of the negative attitudes of the power structure toward their children and themselves. They find it difficult to cope simultaneously with their low economic status and their children's low educational achievement. Obvious inequities within the classroom add to the frustrations of parents and their children, compounding their uncertainties as to the "true" values and purposes of education. In this ambiguous environment, the children of the poor find it difficult to remain in school to acquire skills of a higher level or even to acquire basic skills.

Teachers, too, admit to frustrations in their efforts to teach children. Inexperienced teachers are discouraged by textbooks that they perceive as being too difficult, by curricula they perceive as being too complicated, and by children they regard as "slow," undisciplined, and uninterested in study. That the teachers may not understand the children is another factor aggravating teacher frustration.

When these frustrations lead to rapid teacher turnover, the rapport between teachers and students disintegrates or remains at such a low level that teachers' efforts become ineffective. Under these circumstances, there

---

[12] Ibid., p. 36.

is very little feeling of "community." Before mutual respect is developed and open lines of communication are enjoyed, teachers may be transferred to other work locations or leave the school system.

Students subjected to the classroom of a "temporary" teacher often develop frustrations of their own which may erupt into overt hostility toward the teacher, their peers, or both. It is this overt hostility, ignited by what may be regarded as the smallest pretext, which baffles the middle class and the power structure. The tragedy lies in the larger community's inability to detect the subtle hostility which simmers and finally erupts into destructive acts. The young engage in physical violence or are subjected to psychological damage in far greater proportions than their numbers would indicate.[13] Unfortunately, the minority-poor of our society are those who can least afford destruction in their community and can seldom be expected to recover from it.

Isolation becomes complete when aspiring families do not want to locate in the urban community; new teachers do not want to work in urban community schools; new businesses do not want to invest their money in the community; the government ignores the community until there is another overt eruption of discontent; and members of the community, both young and old, exhibit a deceptive apathy that conceals a turmoil that is unparalleled in the middle-class and affluent communities.[14]

Self-Renewing Proposals

Community Role: Involvement

The reason desegregation programs have failed to escape hostile reactions in some communities and have resulted in violence in others may be due to the lack of previous interactions on issues of common interest between the groups involved. How can we expect one enclave to convince another to agree to bus their children from a comfortable school situation to another school district as part of a social action program supposedly designed to correct some social ill? In particular, how can such expectations be accomplished when the enclaves involved possess attitudes founded upon suspicion and disrespect for each other?

School-community programs should be organized to combat drugs, alcohol, mental health problems, and focus on other issues of common interest and benefit to the total community. Such programs will foster interaction between enclaves, help remove their suspicions, and allow them to

---

[13] Clinard, p. 87.
[14] Ibid., p. 87.

become more informed about the values, perceptions and expectations of each other. In this process, they will be involved collectively in resolving problems that are directly related to the growth and development of their children. Programs of this kind should not be school-centered. They should form a community-centered program involving every urban resource of the school district. Total community involvement will prevent any outside force from placing undue pressure upon the individuals or groups connected with the program.

The curriculum should integrate parents with nonparents who are concerned about the educational system. It is important that the curriculum involve parents who have had children in school and are experienced in coping with the system. The involvement of potential school parents will inform and prepare them for their roles as school parents. This cross-section involvement will increase communication between the different groups of the community and foster more positive mutual attitudes among the diverse groups.

Ideally, the school administration would help organize and work with the parent-teacher associations on the task of providing a good education for students. Properly organized, such associations would serve as catalysts for a human relations program. Similarly, they should serve as a foundation upon which the superintendent and school board members could meet on a regular basis to negotiate the present and future directions of the system.

To accomplish this, superintendents and school board members must get away from merely chatting with parents at school board meetings. It is imperative that they begin getting out into the community and into parents' homes frequently to discuss school–related problems and their solutions. This kind of interaction is vital to any effort that is made to restore public confidence in the public school system. Teachers should also be expected to play an integral part in the development of any school-community programs.

This kind of involvement will foster different attitudes about achieving desegregation and a quality education for every child. By working together, the community's attempts to discuss and develop an acceptable program—involving the desegregation of students, teachers, administrators, and other staff—would seem less threatening.

Community Role: Accountability

When the issue of accountability is raised, we frequently direct our thoughts to teachers, administrators, and school board members. Although this association is correct, it is incomplete unless we include every community member. But even those who agree that accountability is a community concept disagree on how to achieve it.

Three basic characteristics that would maximize accountability within any system are responsibility, commitment, and credibility.

Responsibility may be both extrinsic and intrinsic. Extrinsic responsibility is noninherent; that is, those responsibilities assigned to a person or group are imposed by an outside force. For example, a principal requests that a teacher be at his or her classroom door every day by 8:10 a.m. Here, the teacher has the extrinsic responsibility to report to work by a specific time. The external force is the principal.

Intrinsic responsibility is an inherent phenomenon, that is, those responsibilities that are self-assigned. This assignment carries significant importance because it is directly related to the degree of effectiveness and efficiency with which extrinsic responsibilities are performed. For example, assume that a classroom teacher is given a new curriculum guide. The guide outlines the school district's expectations during the ensuing year. If the teacher does not read or seriously consider the guidelines, then he or she will not feel intrinsically responsible to follow them. At this point, accountability begins to break down because the teacher has assumed a position that does not hold the supervisor accountable. The teacher is unwilling to assume responsibility or is unaware of the supervisor's expectations; he or she then cannot honestly report to the supervisor what effect, positive or negative, the new guidelines have had upon his or her performance or the students' achievement. Not having intrinsically accepted the new extrinsic responsibility, the teacher has become removed from a leadership role and cannot play a positive role in maximizing accountability.

This lack of intrinsic responsibility often creates a situation in which the supervisor criticizes the teacher for unsatisfactory student performance. Since the teacher cannot produce data to show how the new curriculum relates to poor performance, the teacher, in self–defense, cites lack of ability on the part of the students.

If a master teacher or a competent school administrator were to read the above illustration, he or she might raise serious questions concerning certain underlying assumptions. He or she may even become infuriated by the implications that can be drawn from such assumptions. Certain questions should come immediately to the reader's mind. Did the teacher participate in the development of the new curriculum that he or she was expected to use? If there were no supervisory mechanisms which not only encouraged but demanded teacher participation, then it would be unfair to assume the teacher would discover what the school administration expected. The supervisor, consequently, should in no way have expected the teacher to feel intrinsically responsible to follow the guidelines.

Was there an assessment of student capabilities? From the illustration, it is easy to assume that evaluative measures may not have been built in at the outset, or that the mode for the measurement of achievement and performance was not adequately communicated to the teacher. It is vital to the development process that the teacher be totally involved in the evaluative process of the students.

Were the opinions of the students sought? It may not be fully productive to seek the input of upper elementary school pupils, yet they can contribute to their own understanding of what is expected at that level of learning to enhance their analytical skills. On the other hand, the input of secondary school students is vital not only to the students' understanding and growth but also to a realistic assessment of what can and should be incorporated into the evaluation and reorganization aspects of the school curriculum.

Admittedly, the process for curriculum development and delivery frequently excludes teachers, students, and parents. This is too often the reality when teachers are not informed of what they are supposed to teach, when students are not informed of what they are expected to learn, and when parents are not informed of what is expected of their children nor what is expected of them as parents. School districts that still operate in this manner are acknowledging their inability to make the community a living curriculum.

Commitment is closely related to intrinsic responsibility. A teacher, administrator, student, or parent who does not feel the intrinsic responsibility to carry out an extrinsic assignment will not feel committed to specified projects. In this situation, even if an individual carries out an assignment, his or her action will be externally motivated. That is, performance will depend directly upon the external force that created the assignment. Likewise, a person who is committed to carrying out an assignment does feel intrinsic responsibility and performs with less dependence upon external forces.

Credibility is an external phenomenon. It is based upon an extrinsic evaluation of a person's performance: How well is responsibility accepted? It can be argued that a person may carry out extrinsic responsibilities well yet never feel intrinsically responsible for or committed to them. However, a person who is not committed to carrying out extrinsic responsibilities and who does not feel intrinsically responsible for them will, sooner or later, generate public skepticism or a credibility gap regarding the truth of his or her official claims and pronouncements.

Unless responsibility, commitment, and credibility are satisfied, there will always be a hiatus in accountability. In effect, our inability to hold each other accountable is evident in the inadequate education of our urban youth.

What can be done? Perhaps very little at the adult level. Intrinsic attitudes toward responsibility do not easily change after one reaches adulthood. Nevertheless, school-community programs can be developed to focus on a total community accountability system.

The school curriculum (K-12) must begin to reflect this concept of community accountability. Students must be conditioned early in life to the concept of intrinsic responsibility and commitment, and to the feeling of being accountable both to themselves and to their community for the growth and development of each individual, regardless of race, religion, sex, national origin or creed.

Regardless of the methodology advanced to achieve this goal, it is important that students be offered many opportunities to become personally involved in community affairs, using the city as a living curriculum. We must have school and community programs throughout the school curriculum that offer students maximum opportunities to develop attitudes of respect for every person within the community and appreciation for diversity and multiculturalism.

Institutional Role

Regardless of the urban community's role in developing programs to foster new attitudes toward diversity and multiculturalism and to obliterate attitudes that block our youth from a quality education, the community must rely on its institutions. There are many institutions other than the school that play a dominant role in shaping attitudes: the family, church, and other agencies in the private and public sectors. Many attitudes are reflected through institutions that shape a community.

As technology continues to rip at the seams of family structure, the family appears to have a diminished institutional influence in role development. Consequently, schools are having to assume functions once thought to be in the purview of the family. Regardless of what the future may hold for the family as an institution, it is imperative that urban schools continue to integrate the family into their total curriculum.

Since present-day students will constitute the families of tomorrow, the urban school curriculum should have a comprehensive, ongoing program that focuses upon the family function in the community and its role in the educational development of its children. Any program related to the family unit should incorporate the entire family. Schools should have a human relations project as part of the total curriculum—from the kindergarten to the home. Such a program would help students develop attitudes that foster respect and appreciation for their fellow students and nurture concern for the welfare of every person within their community. The lack of such attitudes has prevented the urban community from resolving the issues of integration, desegregation, discrimination, and racism.

Before we can live and work together in harmony in the same community, we must build a community together. In order to accomplish this, a healthy mental foundation must exist, characterized by positive attitudes and respect for one another. The development of such a foundation must begin in early childhood and continue throughout the educational life of the child. Each student must be given many opportunities to become personally involved in an ongoing family-community human relations program. The Institute for Urban Education and Human Resource Development proposed in Chapter Five is an excellent medium through which to develop a curriculum design for such a program.

It would be presumptuous to suggest that the family and school can or should take on this mammoth developmental program without the assistance of the church and other agencies in the community.

The church is one of the most segregated institutions in our society. Its primary function is to promote its own welfare, to maintain and preserve its doctrines and traditions, many of which are discriminatory and racist in nature. Many religions are in conflict with the promotion of such concepts as interreligious exchange, interracial relations, integration and desegregation. This conflict becomes even more complex when students, because of their own sectarian experiences, adopt attitudes of disrespect for certain groups of people, particularly minority groups.

Although the black church has traditionally played a great role in the black struggle for freedom, it has not and is not playing the role it should in the education of its youth.

Notwithstanding these circumstances, the school district must urge churches to participate in a school-community human relations program and other programs that will penetrate the racial and segregated barriers within the urban community. The school district must reach out and strongly encourage its minority churches to become active, totally involved and committed to the education of its youth.

What kind of programs are we proposing? Within every urban school there are a few teachers who would volunteer to work with churches within the community to organize tutorial programs. However, this is assuming that in every church there are a few volunteers who would accept the responsibility of giving up one evening, two hours per week, to tutor. The volunteer teachers would periodically run training workshops for the volunteer tutors. Some of the volunteer tutors could be talented secondary school students. Families who avail themselves of the tutorial service must have someone from the family unit volunteering service to the program as a tutor or as a supervisor.

The school district might encourage and assist urban churches to set up summer school seminars for students who have fallen behind. It should work with the churches to find health services for the handicapped within the community.

These are only a few areas where the school and church can work together in school-community related programs. Logistics, of course, would have to be worked out in order to implement such programs. Where in the community will they be held? Who will coordinate each program? Will there be a financial cost? If so, who will finance it? The Institute proposed in Chapter Five considers coordinating resources to resolve these logistics. As the consciousness of parents and the church community is raised, participants will begin to accept greater responsibility among themselves for providing such services for their youth.

During the past ten years, the citizens of many urban areas have elected black mayors. In many of these cities, the racial composition of school boards and city councils consists of a black majority or a large minority representation. Whereas this representation implies to many that minorities have made great strides, others recognize that it has inherited the ruins left by its predecessors.

As soon as the political power of urban areas began to change from white to black control, a great exodus of white families began. Businesses started to uproot and expand outside the city limits, leaving behind blocks of vacant buildings. The result of this exodus is an eroded property tax base: the tax base upon which the urban schools rely for 80 percent of their revenue.

In order to save the urban community, the private sector has an important developmental role to play and must be given opportunities to help develop attitudinal changes within the urban community. Members of the private sector should be encouraged to work with urban institutes such as the one developed in Chapter Five.

We will find no one disagreeing that federal, state, and local agencies can contribute to improving human relations within the urban community. Differences in opinion arise when we attempt to determine how they can contribute.

Our national security depends upon how well we as a nation live together. Since urban communities are the nuclei of this nation, it is vital to the survival of all that we be concerned about the behavior and attitudes prevalent in each community. If federal, state, and local governments are concerned about human relations, they should reflect their concern through national, state, and local policies. If they are not aware of the relationship between our survival, attitudes, and respect for one another, then urban school officials across the nation should join forces to create such an awareness.

However, before federal and state governments financially support urban community human relations programs, they should closely evaluate whether or not such programs maximize community involvement. Government agencies should explore the kinds of supportive structures that are provided by local governments and other agencies. The school district and local government should be made to demonstrate that they have a fully integrated program that encompasses the total urban community, one that ranges from the classroom to the home. Urban communities that are willing to design and promote a community-wide, integrated human relations program should receive financial assistance from federal and state governments. Once the program is in operation, the state revenue formula should be adjusted to guarantee the program annual funding. This is not to suggest that federal funding should not be continued, but it is important that the program's survival not be totally dependent upon federal subsidy.

Federal and state governments should make sure that the funds given to the community are not wasted or ill-managed as they were during the 1960's and early 1970's. It is important that a strong, ongoing evaluation program be instituted to monitor the program and the use of the funds. Recipients of funds should not be allowed to evaluate themselves.

We have reached a time in our quest for human survival when it has become important for us to examine more closely our behavior and attitudes. What happened in our urban communities during the 1960's and 1970's awakened us to the fact that we must be concerned about the lives of all our citizens. But it is not yet clear to us whether the masses in this country realize that national and world survival depend upon our collective national ability to develop respect and appreciation for each group within our multiethnic, multicultural society.

Since attitudes develop early in life, urban schools must introduce them in the primary-grade curriculum, through a program that continues throughout the public school experience of the child. Again, such programs should encourage the participation of the church and the family, and should reach every agency and member of the community.

The urban community must become a living curriculum if we expect to correct the attitudinal problems that are interfering with the educational progress of the urban child.

2
Urban Educational Leadership
Clement B.G. London

Prevailing Circumstances

Our schools are in trouble. Public confidence in institutions of all varieties is seriously eroded. We are in a period of transformation in American society, when the quality of services and products is under heavy criticism. Many people feel that they are not getting a fair return on their expenditures and are losing confidence in the people providing products and services.

The schools have not escaped the quality-decline and lack-of-confidence criticism. The back-to-basics movement, declining test scores, tax referendum failures, and an abundance of news articles on the way schools are failing to meet student needs are current examples of the declining confidence in public education.

Trends in education generally reflect the philosophy of a vocal or influential segment of society. All too often, however, the interpretation of events is limited to what newspapers say or what is found in surveys of school practices among educators. On the other hand, an analysis of educational literature as a basis for determining trends is limited only to guidelines set by the analyst.

A recent survey [1] measured the attitudes of Americans towards their public schools and identified ten critical problems facing public schools in our nation: (1) lack of discipline, (2) use of drugs, (3) lack of proper financial support, (4) integration/segregation/busing, (5) poor curriculum/poor standards, (6) lack of good teachers, (7) size of schools/classes, (8) pupils' lack of interest, (9) crime/vandalism, and (10) parents' lack of interest.

Disruption and unrest in schools, like other prevailing problems, have roots deep within the fabric of our society and its educational systems. The

[1] George Gallup, "The 10th Annual Gallup Poll of the Public's Attitudes Toward the Public Schools," *Phi Delta Kappan* 60 (September 1978): 33-45.

major problems of American society are reflected in its schools and in the lives of young people. Teenagers themselves have raised some very serious concerns about the effects of questionable behavior of persons holding positions of authority. They have lived with the pain of poverty and the guilt of affluence, with racism's corrosion of relationships between white and non-white peoples, and with the constraining effects of adult-run bureaucracies. Young people are restive with this disillusionment and with their needs for change, increased liberty, and relevance for their lives; they are restive because of society's frequent estrangement from its young people in general.

Our schools are a vulnerable and accessible focus for some of these disaffections. They also heighten and trigger such issues in particularly volatile ways. Students' concerns with society and schools are always present, but they gain public attention when expressed in ways that disrupt orderly school processes.

The current state of public schools poses a great many unanswered questions. Hopefully, continuing research might help us to not only find out what the real problems are, but more specifically and significantly, how they may be honestly addressed. Addressing this single issue may indeed take concerned persons into the basic area of racism which, incidentally, does not constitute one of the basic problems identified by George Gallup, but which affects all of the others.

One overriding question hovers above the endless debate on contemporary educational issues. This question concerns the issues of the structure, delivery, and outcome of educational goods and services now and in the foreseeable future.

If schools are to cope with the problems arriving in ever-increasing numbers on their doorsteps, then their response will have to be much more than piecemeal, much more than remedial. Unfortunately, "remedial" has become a code word signifying the hasty infusion of money into programs which are designed to operate after the fact. These programs are not preventive nor are they widely effective. In fact, they must, for the most part, maintain failure in order to justify their own existence.

Therefore, "remedial" programs or other piecemeal, superficial treatment becomes, in the long run, an exercise in futility. It is inimical to structured progress and counter-productive in scope. It is very much like what Ronald Berman calls swatting mosquitoes in order to prevent yellow fever. The main idea should be to drain the swamps, not to create little islands of security under the netting.[2]

---

[2] Ronald Berman, "Stamping Out Illiteracy," *Chronicle of Higher Education,* XVII (2 October 1978): 72.

Nothing short of a comprehensive program seems sufficient to address the crucial conditions which beset public schools. As educators attempt to critically examine conditions in terms of conflicting demands which are placed on schools, they are forced to confront the basic issue of how they can effectuate change and turn the ebb of cynicism into a flow of confidence.

According to Harold Shane,[3] the task of dealing with these persistent issues must become one of tooling up for the fundamental reorganization of content, structure, administrative policy, and teacher education. The call for social and political changes and the plea for new educational leadership made in the 1960's and early 1970's [4] seem to echo and become more urgent today. Perhaps the purpose of public schools holds the key to how they function.

The Purpose of Public Schools

From colonial times, the American people have had an abiding faith in the power of education. Educational programs developed through the schools have been a major factor in providing an enlightened citizenry, in making self-government work, in creating national unity out of diversity, in integrating immigrants and their children into the American way of life, and in teaching the philosophical equality of all persons.[5]

Assuming that this has been the established function of schools, current circumstances seem to require a re-establishment of the schools' original purpose. In this sense, schools must reassert their commitment to the highest ideals; they must teach all of the basics and a great deal more to all learners of all ages; they must attempt to address educational ills; and they must learn to do it all at a reasonable cost.[6] But these ideals, however noble, must be examined in the light of current circumstances which relate to an environment that greatly differs from that of colonial times. The time span between periods is characterized by a shift from an agrarian to a highly technological society and from sparse rural living to mass urban liv-

---

[3] Harold G. Shane, *Curriculum Change Toward the Twenty-first Century* (Washington, D.C.: National Education Association, 1977), p. 91.

[4] *See* ASCD, *Leadership for Improving Instruction, 1960 Yearbook* (Washington, D.C.: Association for Supervision and Curriculum Development, 1960), and Ronald C. Doll, *Leadership to Improve Schools* (Worthington, Ohio: Charles A. Jones, 1972).

[5] *See* Lawrence Cremin, *The Transformation of the School: Progressivism in America, 1876-1957* (New York: Alfred A. Knopf, 1961), and Lawrence Cremin, *The Genius of American Education* (New York: Vintage Books, 1965).

[6] Arthur Hope, "Critical Realities in School and Society," *Improving the Human Condition,* ed. James J. Jelinek (Washington, D.C.: Association for Supervision and Curriculum Development, 1978), pp. 1-28.

ing. The complexities which generate new demands, needs, and interests inevitably call for drastic changes in the concept and organization of education, as well as in the delivery of educational goods and services. Indeed, they require a re-evaluation and reinterpretation of the purposes of schools.

Several trends emerged in the evolutionary process of American education from colonial times to the present. From the private system of colonial education, the school has been transfigured into a fifty-state system of public education and indigenous development of private education.[7]

Undergirding the phenomenal variety and scope of educational offerings are two questions which must be repeatedly addressed: Who shall be educated? Is education in America really meant for all of the children of all the people? The debate that persists around these issues includes constructive as well as biting criticism.

Butts talks of a moral authority which should reinforce the fundamental objectives of schooling. He reasons that the priority of curriculum should center around those values which constitute the base of the American civic creed of liberty, equality, and justice.[8] For Clark, the function should include for all children the democratic beliefs, ideas, and patterns of behavior which are consistent with personal and social stability.[9]

Hope sees the role of the schools as unique. Its central function, its charge from society, is the education of its members, particularly the young, in such a fashion that they may live in harmony with themselves, with each other, and with their environments. Included therein should be the scope that will allow them to pursue their various purposes and to solve their different problems with maximum regard for the freedom of each individual and for the collective welfare of all.[10]

The push to urbanization and modernization; the need for global outreach and improved understanding; and relationships of local, national, and international dimensions have prescribed the function of the school. Thus, Randolph considers it the role of the school to provide training in analytical thinking and to bring the future into what we do in the schools. She makes a plea for the inclusion of future consequences in the personal awareness of the young to help them develop their reflective, rational skills

---

[7] Ronald C. Doll, *Curriculum Improvement: Decision Making and Process* (Boston: Allyn and Bacon, 1978), p. 7.

[8] R. Freeman Butts, *"The Public School as Moral Authority,"* ed. R. Freeman Butts and others. (Washington, D.C.: Association for Supervision and Curriculum Development, 1977), pp. 5-20.

[9] Kenneth B. Clark, *Prejudice and Your Child* (Boston: Beacon Press, Inc., 1966), p. 5.

[10] Hope, pp. 1-28.

for engaging in cogent decisions that transcend the material gratification of a free enterprise technology.[11]

For some, schools are seen as systems linked to other larger systems in a social structure. Campbell defines the schools as examples of institutions designed to serve particular social purposes. They are social systems linked to the broader society through formal structures of government, with defined units possessing governmental responsibilities, and serving as a means for legitimizing educational policies.[12]

A rational conclusion, drawn from these several philosophical stances, is that they and their educational programs should derive their legitimacy from the production of a literate citizenry. However, considerable challenges continue to grow from a clear recognition that the system of public education is grossly deficient, some teachers are not teaching, many pupils are not achieving, and numerous organizations lack the capacity for adaptability.

These conditions are causing an increasing number of citizens to insist on the schools being held accountable for their procedures and products. This is nothing new; it is, however, an insistence which is accompanied by harsh criticism. Adams, for example, charges that schools are doing their job; that public schools, particularly in urban communities, are doing precisely what they are designed to do: that is, to transmit cultural heritage and to facilitate the socialization process. He argues, however, that this cultural heritage is one of racism and that urban schools, especially those in poor neighborhoods, function in a way which ensures that there will always be busboys, dishwashers, and other low-level functioning persons for the privileged to look down upon.[13]

Adams considers this situation to be calculated, that stereotyping and rationalizations are offered to cover up failure, inability, or the refusal to produce the desired effects in students. Thus, one may observe a segment of society sailing along in its lifeboat, preferring to pass its preferential educational existence, and watching the less privileged drown in a sea of ignorance, lack of power, and disgrace.

Bowles and Gintis relate the school situation to a production orientation framework. They maintain that the repressive and unequal aspects of

---

[11] Elizabeth Randolph, Foreword to *Improving the Human Condition,* ed. James J. Jelinek (Washington, D.C.: Association for Supervision and Curriculum Development, 1978), pp. v-vi.

[12] Roald F. Campbell and others, *The Organization and Control of American Schools,* 2nd ed. (Columbus, Ohio: Charles E. Merrill Publishing Company, 1970), p. 11.

[13] Frank Adams, "Highland Folk School: Getting Information, Going Back and Teaching It," *Harvard Educational Review,* Reprint Series, No. 10 (1976), pp. 96-163.

public schooling derive their purpose from the need to supply a large, cheap labor force which is compatible with the social relations of the capitalist production of economic goods.[14]

The argument follows that in the present educational system, public schools reflect the inherently unequal structure of our capitalist economy. The system fosters and rewards behaviors which are desired by business and industry so that getting ahead in schools, as in society, depends a great deal on parental wealth and race. Therefore, the present educational system functions in a manner which has not, does not, and cannot provide equality of educational opportunity.

Friedenberg takes a similar stance in his assessment of the function of the school system.[15] He sees economics as the basis of the national state's incapacity to deal generously with the less fortunate. His argument is that technological development has led, instead, to a greater concentration of wealth. He criticizes, for example, the constant argument raised against the thrust for a guaranteed annual income. Friedenberg notes that every proposal is met by querulous objections that if the income were large enough to insure a decent life, it would no longer be possible to get people to accept the worst and the most poorly paid jobs.

Friedenberg sees a connection between the economic and educational conditions. He concludes that a major function of the compulsory public school system is to conceal the functioning of the social class system by purporting to equalize economic opportunity; to convey a false model of the workings of the political and economic systems; and to humiliate the children of the poor into believing that they are too dumb to do anything effective to change society. The traditional defense of beleaguered school personnel is that the locus of difficulty for the poor is not the schools, but the family, the neighborhoods, and society.

Michael Katz has reasoned that public schools have, since their establishment, served as instruments for freezing the low status of the urban areas' most oppressed groups. They do this through a traditional stratifying system of fixing the social status of people, sorting young people, locating winners and losers, and directing students into appropriate places in the job hierarchy. This arrangement fits in with the logic of an already stratified society. Therefore, the school system is seen as having been organized to perpetuate class stratification and exploitation.[16]

[14] Samuel Bowles and Herbert Gintis, *Schooling in Capitalist America: Educational Reform and the Contradictions of Economic Life* (New York: Basic Books, 1975), pp. 3-17.

[15] Edgar Z. Friedenberg, *The Disposal of Liberty and Other Industrial Wastes* (New York: Doubleday, 1976), pp. 1-27.

[16] Michael Katz, *Class Bureaucracy and Schools* (New York: Praeger Publishers, 1971), pp. xiii-xxvi.

Less caustic criticism comes from Colin Greer, whose thesis is a recognition that schools have serviced all lower-class people in the same manner; that it is simply the fate of history that the more recent comers to the urban areas happen to be nonwhite; and that, essentially, the factors of control and maintenance of the status quo remain inherently entrenched in governance and in the delivery system of educational goods and services.[17]

A more reasonable function of public schools would be to make it possible for all children, regardless of background and scholastic aptitude, to acquire adequate levels of skills in reading, writing, and practical arithmetic.[18] The means to do this are already available or are becoming available through careful training. There should be no doubt that if training opportunities were available, poor people would take advantage of them. Of course, such training would not necessarily lead to social equality for poor people, but it could certainly do more than any mild educational treatment could do, and perhaps as much as can be done in any way that respects the right of people to be different.

One critical concern is not whether the schools will compensate for hardships inflicted on the mass poor, but rather, whether they will cease to degrade and demoralize low-income children, thus destroying their enthusiasm and motivation and thwarting their belief in the schools as a possible way out of poverty.

What education does for the individual is one thing; what it does for society is another. The public looks to education to solve social problems by changing people. It does not work very well because problems of human behavior are generally better dealt with by changing incentives.

The publics served by the common school have always been multiple and pluralistic. An important difference between then and now is that until recently these publics, at least those who controlled the schools, co-operated towards a common goal of molding diversity into unity. Today some important publics are withdrawing from the public school arena.

Tucker's forecast in 1971 was that, to the extent that these newly concerned publics value pluralism over uniformity, and to the degree that public schools cannot adjust to the new demands, we can expect to witness an increasing flight from public schools.[19] The implications of this trend

[17] Colin Greer, *The Great School Legend* (New York: Basic Books, 1972), pp. vii-xiii.

[18] Carl Bereiter, "Must We Educate?" *Curriculum Handbook* (Boston: Allyn and Bacon, Inc., 1977), pp. 374-381.

[19] Jan L. Tucker, "Challenges to the Common School: Implications for Curriculum," *Confronting Curriculum Reform,* ed. Elliott E. Eisener (Boston: Little, Brown and Co., Inc., 1971), pp. 17-48.

tend to boggle the mind. Perhaps we are not well-equipped to handle the problems precisely because they are economic, political, social, as well as emotional and cognitive.

It may imply therefore, that meaningful strategies for educational change must embrace a transformation of the mechanism of power and privilege in the economic sphere.[20] This transformation must be inclusive of national societal considerations, because any change in education which is predicated on a patchwork curriculum and narrow school policy is fraught with difficulties. It is a simplistic approach to very complex problems. The outcome of all meaningful educational change is, after all, social change, and this implies change in people, their perceptions and behaviors.

Most people have been committed to the view that public schools are the cornerstone of education in a democratic society. College and university schools of education have been developed to serve and promote this end. Thus, the challenges to public schools also present a real threat to the values of professionals who are asked to assume new leadership roles and initiate curriculum change.

Curriculum Change Through Leadership

Curriculum reform is not enough. The alarming slide into mediocrity in academic achievement will be far more difficult to reverse than suggested by recent headlines announcing curriculum reform. Until the deep ramifications of political, social, and economic considerations are addressed in a realistic way and dealt with directly, today's popular curriculum movement, however well conceived and intentioned, may become an exercise in the application of cosmetics.

Comprehensive change must come from dynamic leadership. Leadership in education must come from highly competent persons who believe in democracy, the potentialities inherent in people, and the significance of the educational process. Leadership must come from those who have the knowledge, insights, abilities, and skills needed to function successfully as recognized educational leaders in helping people identify, analyze, and solve the problems with which they and society are confronted.[21]

This leadership must provide an orientation grounded in the belief in the capability of the individual to transform and transcend his immediate environment. Such a philosophical stance implies a commitment to human

---

[20] Herbert Gintis, "Toward a Political Economy of Education: A Radical Critique of Ivan Illich's Deschooling Society," *Harvard Educational Review*, Reprint Series, No. 10 (1976), pp. 7-34.

[21] Edgard L. Morphet and others, *Educational Administration: Concepts, Practices and Issues* (Englewood Cliffs, N.J.: Prentice Hall, Inc., 1964), p. vi.

liberation through a distribution of power whereby individuals can partici-pate interdependently in determining the direction of their lives. In schools, this commitment calls for teachers, students, and others to become partici-pants in a dynamic mutual process of action and reflection, rather than one of mere passive transmission or reception of prepackaged knowledge.

Schools have reciprocal relationships with society as a whole; they not only exert influence, but have influence over many of the forces exerted upon them. Schools, in the opinion of Macekura, are the children of the community, fathered and mothered by all of its dreams and hopes, and bred by the frustrations and hopelessness in the hearts of its citizens.[22] By their very nature, schools mirror the social climate. Therefore, it is when social institutions such as schools grow obsolete that they fail to serve the needs of the people, and it is then the responsibility of the public to update them.

The public can accomplish this in a number of ways: by direct par-ticipation in the processes of change, delegating this responsibility to a consortia of professionals, or doing it jointly. Participation by consum-ers of public school education—students, parents, and community residents —represents the emergence of important publics who wield an enormous amount of energy. These new energy sources can combine their skills with those of professionals to help generate fundamental reform in public school education.

In practical terms, this means preparing students not only for jobs but for work that must be done, especially in small, urban-oriented business enterprises, in commerce, industry and government. The ecology of the urban environment is replete with services and resources in the private and public sectors which must become viable components and extensions of schools.

Mobilization of Resources

A dichotomous situation exists in education. It is reflected in the realm of what is ideal and what is real—that is, what the schools ought to be doing and what they are indeed doing. Continuing criticism and evaluation signals a healthy recognition that there is always a need for adjustment and improvement, and that change, whenever it comes, must be consistent with past, current, and projected states of the human condition.

Current research supports the view of the complexity of educational problems and the need to deal with the possible, beginning at the local level. John Goodlad, for example, in a preliminary report on recent

---

[22] Joseph Macekura, "Building Discipline in a 'Tough' School," *Social Education* 42 (February 1978): 98-104.

findings of his eight-year study, "Schooling in America," has this to say: "I was right in asserting that schools are complex, unique cultures, and we had better seek to understand them better before we try to change them." [23]

A rapprochement may derive its strength, legitimacy and significance from a realistic view of past accomplishments and future possibilities. This rapprochement must address population trends, favor socioeconomic considerations, and facilitate the relevant relationships among schools and other educational institutions at the local level, with support from district, state, and federal governments. These factors provide a set of interlocking relationships which influence schools.

A recent projection suggests that a majority of the world's population will live in cities or towns by the end of the century.[24] Here at home, seven out of ten people already live in cities; the problems which affect education are, indeed, largely problems of urban orientation and needs. We are thus challenged to fundamentally change schooling to reflect relevance of substance in relation to time and place; to see and understand the school as an institution in relation to the larger ecological mosaic of which it forms an integral part.

Despite the incidence of rapid mobility, the shift in population, and changing lifestyles, we are learning that there will be fewer students of college age in the immediate future, and that fewer students will study philosophy, literature and classics. Instead, larger proportions will study nursing, business, engineering, and other service-related courses. Also, the category of young people aged 14-22 will decline.[25] This means, of course, increasing competition for students among universities. Many school personnel are convinced that colleges must offer more courses that are vocationally relevant if they are to succeed in that competition.[26]

America's colleges and universities are challenged to respond in diverse ways to a common new urgency of reviewing what and how youth are being taught on their campuses. Faced with declining enrollments, dissatisfied with student fitness for academic work, and feeling outside pressures to make diplomas relevant to job demands, school personnel are forced to

[23] John I. Goodlad, "A Preview of 'Schooling in America'" (Harold Shane Interviews John Goodlad), *Phi Delta Kappan* 60 (September 1978): 47-50.

[24] Ed Brown, "Underdevelopment Economies: An Alternative View," *The Black Collegian* 9 (September/October 1978): 38-44.

[25] Peter O'Brien, "Urban Education—Whither," *Urban, Social and Educational Issues,* eds. Leonard Golubchick and Berry Persky, 2nd ed. (Dubuque, Iowa: Kendall/Hunt Publishing Co., 1974), pp. 1-4.

[26] Christopher J. Hurn, "The Reemergence of Liberal Education," *Change* 10 (October 1978): 8-9.

re-examine the current content of classes and approaches to educating students.

The critical situation has become more acute because of the drastic cutback in educational development programs. Arising from the efforts of minority recruiters and from open admissions policies (both appropriately labeled as equal access measures), developmental programs have been designed for students at the lower achievement levels and for those with nontraditional academic talents or nontraditional goals.[27] In light of dwindling student bodies and teacher surplus, developmental programs in colleges and universities across the country not only face a drop in enrollment but a shortage of teachers.

As one moves from the college level to that of the public schools, a much larger issue surfaces. The distribution of population and widespread adherence to neighborhood school policies mean that student bodies are often segregated by socioeconomic characteristics as well as race. Generally speaking, the socioeconomic status of a student body reflects the education, occupation, and income of the adults in the community.

Some high schools in high-income neighborhoods, for instance, offer virtually no vocational preparation because it is assumed that almost all of their students will go on to college. Many lower-income schools are less likely to offer advanced courses in mathematics and foreign languages than their suburban counterparts. Stereotypical assumptions and low expectations which are based on social class, race, and achievement, frequently interfere with educational decisions and the delivery process. There is also evidence that many urban teachers prefer to teach in middle- and upper-income schools. As a consequence, teachers with experience and seniority often transfer from schools located in lower-income areas, leaving younger and relatively inexperienced teachers to provide most of the instruction for lower-income students.[28]

Are these acts not an abrogation of the ethical component of the professional code? Are there ethical and moral standards for checkmating these behaviors? There ought to be! A call for the exercise of a moral consciousness is consistent with the current global concern for morality and basic human rights. If agents of educational change are serious about their assertions and expressed commitments, they must assume the responsibility and demonstrate their concern by first recognizing all persons from a humanistic frame of reference. Opportunities must be created so that each citizen

---

[27] Mack Faite, "More Teachers for Educational Development Programs," *Improving the Human Condition,* ed. James J. Jelinek (Washington, D.C.: Association for Supervision and Curriculum Development, 1978), pp. 212-213.

[28] Campbell, pp. 304-305.

can develop to his fullest capacity. Inequities serve only to stultify the growth of the individual and, consequently, of the nation.

Education must assume a modified process of socialization and preparation for the real world. Ethical preachments from podiums become hollow and hypocritical if action fails to match words. If curriculum and instruction set goals for narrow careers, students will perceive their role model in a narrow career; when educators are indifferent, biased, or the purveyors of purely technocratic solutions to vital problems, our potentially most creative students will reflect these approaches.

Interpersonal relationships take on particular meaning when hopes for social change and scope for improving the human condition can coalesce around relevant action. Educational leadership must proceed from an optimistic frame of reference. They must possess the insight, knowledge, and understanding to convince youngsters that there is no doubt that every individual has something great to offer. It requires constant effort to recognize every favorable aspect of the student and to then reinforce all positive attributes, no matter how small.

The importance of the mobilization and deployment of educational resources is a critical issue. Inequitable distribution of resources must give way to the import of the democratic process. The improvement of the human condition should become the special concern of those who are responsible for the educational resources that affect curriculum and teaching. It is the responsibility of every person and organization involved with educational change to see that the direction of the change is towards the greater good of man and his environment.

To accord the courtesy of privileges to a preferred section of the population is to contradict the essence of American democracy. It constitutes an abrogation of the moral and civil rights of others less favored.

Among the undeniable and most urgent responsibilities of the school is the requirement of presenting a wide variety of relevant opportunities in school life to stimulate students to participate meaningfully and succeed. The result must be a reasonable preparation for survival in a changing technological environment. Thus, teachers must like what they do and have positive feelings for all children. Regardless of the subject area taught, successful teachers should demonstrate certain sparks of enthusiasm which capture the imagination of each student and increase the student's motivation to learn.

In the final analysis, the responsibility rests with the classroom teacher, and the success or failure of any educational program depends upon the teacher's judgment and performance. Whether the curriculum treats the basics of reading, writing, and numbering, or is more sophisticated, it is the teacher who will have to translate subject matter into actuality.

Therefore, there is a need for teachers who know these skills well and attempt to practice them for themselves and with their students. There is a need for teachers who care about students; who seek an understanding of their abilities, homelife, special interests and problems; who demonstrate their caring in scores of specific tangible acts; and who insist on the ingredients of disciplined classrooms in which the teaching-learning act can best be facilitated.

Ideals and Realities of Education

Schools can and do work. Public education and leadership flourish where circumstances provide the necessary congeniality and nurturing. They require more than a will-to-do; certainly they include a spirit of cooperation and expertise, even when lacking other essential features. Yet they flourish, some more than others. What is it among the leadership of some schools, their educational packages and delivery systems that works well? A look at some specifics should provide a point of reference for viewing the real in relation to the ideal in schools, curriculum, and educational leadership.

There continues to be a great deal of negative criticism about public school education. One can identify a multiplicity of circumstances which affect public criticism. One can also add others to the list of problems identified by the Gallup study, such as change, progress and complexity; issues of power, politics and protection; rationalizations and excuses for performance or a lack of it; and problems of accountability, shared governance, resources, and financing for the support of programs.

The list can support continuing criticism. Criticizing is a healthy, democratic act, but there is need for criticism that offers constructive suggestion for change. This, too, is taking place simultaneously, although not with the same degree of emphasis. Reports feature past and contemporary studies of schools and educational leaders struggling for educational excellence. Educational literature occasionally carries success stories of schools and teachers meeting the need for improved programs. Often the levels of achievement are quite exemplary. So, despite overwhelming negative criticism, hope is generated in many schools across the nation. The problem remains, however, that the force of negative criticism is so profound that it all but overshadows the positive. Reports on achievements are often paled by such adverse criticism.

Isolated success stories in education invariably serve to reassure the nation's belief in the efficacy of mass public education. These stories also serve to show that schools can and do work. Not only must we strive for continued educational success, we must be aware that success is happening under the guidance of good leadership in sundry places, even without ideal conditions.

It seems justifiable that attention be given to an examination of some successful schools. Much may be learned from them—their reason for being and their mission of academic and operational excellence. One may at least derive a sense of the dynamism of leadership which helps to promulgate such outstanding educational achievement.

Success Schools: What are They Doing Right?

In a recent report on case studies of successful schools, Arlene Silberman [29] brought to public attention a discussion of three specific cases drawn from a wide selection of schools throughout the United States. For the most part, these schools met the challenges which others offer as excuses for failure—failure which comes on the heels of rationalizations for the inability to perform.

Associated with these three cases are the following issues of leadership: a lack of sufficient funds, the stereotypical response that schools in disadvantaged areas must accept lower academic standards and social promotions, and the notion that there is little that ordinary individuals such as parents can do to improve education.

The survey found numerous schools throughout the nation operating in a successful manner that contradicts general rationalizations for failure. The success of these schools is characterized by their effectiveness, despite the engulfing odds that many educators claim interfere with their efforts to provide genuine leadership.

On the issue of insufficient money, the Eastbrook Elementary School in Seminole County near Orlando, Florida, is cited as a prime example which dispels the myth that money buys good schools. By operating with a spartan budget well beneath the state's average, this school has combined faculty commitment with profound educational theory, translated into clear educational goals, practical planning, and careful effectuation. To provide a viable curriculum package for teaching and learning, this school has combined the best of traditional and progressive education, stressing the three R's while encouraging personal initiative.

All of these factors are supported by the strong motivation of a concerned faculty whose belief in the promise of its students is reflected in the delivery of educational services beyond contractual limitations of time. Frances Walton, the principal of Eastbrook Elementary School, observes that "the parking lot fills up early and empties late."

---

[29] Arlene Silberman, "Schools That Work," *Reader's Digest,* June 1978, pp. 55-61.

In the second case, the issue of educational leadership challenges the rationalization that schools in disadvantaged areas must accept low academic standards. Captain Arthur Roth Elementary School in Cleveland, Ohio, is cited. Located in a poverty area, the school's student body is substantially Black. Yet this school is so academically successful that families have been known to falsify their addresses so their children could qualify for admission.

The principal, Barbara Eggleston, and her faculty shun defeatist attitudes and establish high expectations for the students. They expect success and they get it through hard and honest toil. By working together, learning from each other's strengths, and shoring up others' weaknesses, the teachers have become dynamic decision-makers who determine objectives and develop programs with a combined expertise, zeal, and commitment that has resulted in the dramatic upswing of their students' national standardized test scores in mathematics and reading.

A third case in point refutes the assumption that there is little that ordinary individuals—parents or teachers—can do when faced with overwhelming educational problems. Dubbed the school of "great need" in 1973-1974, the Rios Elementary School in San Diego has since triumphed over its handicaps of low reading and mathematics scores, severe overcrowding, rough discipline problems, low staff morale and poor attendance from a student body drawn from the area's lowest socioeconomic level, to become a model school. This is the result of dynamic educational leadership.

Basic to American democratic principles is the element of consistency. This is often reflected in the fundamental use of choices and in the right to options. If it is argued that the cases cited here are exceptional, it may be necessary to call attention to the fact that hundreds of such schools are in successful operation. These prototypes indicate that there are in fact mechanisms at work producing successful educational experiences worthy of emulation.

There are other instances of successful educational leadership in more diverse settings and under traditional and nontraditional circumstances. One might, for example, wish to look at a successful open classroom model such as the Willston Central School in rural Vermont. A quality public school, its success is generated by patient, cooperative leadership which ensures pleasant and exciting educational experiences through hard work and specific goals.

There are schools with programs which attempt to accommodate all students. Their purpose is to provide an education that ensures their students of becoming literate and functioning individuals. There are schools, too, which redirect failure-prone youth toward earning worthwhile diplomas. Others, such as Fairfield High School in Fairfield, California, have strong leadership goals, operate with solid academic course work, and therefore foster dramatic improvement in SAT scores.

The foundation of this success is the full support and involvement of students and parents, as well as the faculty's positive expectations of students, based on the basic belief in their students' abilities. Motivation, ability, and hard work supplement the success picture.

One can peruse the literature and find the list extending to include public schools with winning test scores and curriculum emphasizing the classics, schools who teach the basics or allow students to earn college-level credits. These schools range from kindergarten through the 12th grade; they are found in rural, urban, and suburban settings, and may be designated as "magnet," alternative, or nontraditional public schools.

Educational Leadership at Work

The success dramatized by these case studies points to important factors regarding the crucial nature of educational leadership. Generally speaking, they raise questions about such issues as school size, staff expertise, preparation, commitment, accountability, cooperation, and shared governance. The model schools have utilized good, tested, traditional educational methods and practices. Their staffs have worked conscientiously. But, more than that, the leadership offered by both district and school administrations in general and by principals in particular is professional and cooperative.

The leadership of a school is critical to its success. In each instance, the leadership has worked in a concerted way with its community. A key factor in its success has been the dramatized insistence that parents and educators become collaborative planners and decision-makers in their community schools. They plan programs, evaluate results, and share the successes.

Inherent in this leadership and its collaboration is the school itself, which is viewed as a social system. In terms of social systems theory, the model schools may be considered as complexes of interactive and dynamic systems. Structurally, the schools are unique systems within the hierarchy of superordinate, parallel, and subordinate relationships of the larger social system, the school district. This hierarchy of relationships is the focus for allocating and intergrating personnel and material to achieve the goals of the system.

Operationally, however, the administration of the school always functions within a network of person-to-person interaction. Thus, the nature of these interpersonal, social relationships becomes a control factor in the administration of the schools.[30] The principals of the success schools have, by reason of their performance, subscribed to the profundity of sound educational theory. As leaders, principals must initiate the appropriate structures within schools. This is necessary for orchestrating the functions of teachers, guidance counselors, and other student personnel specialists.

Of particular interest is the fact that the model schools have set the tone and provided the motivation to generate success. Thus, when an inner-city school with students of supposedly below-average achievement, and a suburban school with below-average funding both succeed academically, there is room for faith in public school education. When, for example, a school which seemed deficient in almost every aspect turns itself around completely in a short time, there is further evidence that ordinary people can do extraordinary things.

The success of these schools and hundreds of other unreported successes clearly indicate that whatever is basically wrong with the public school system can be remedied with intelligent planning and thoughtful and committed teachers working in collaboration with informed and concerned parents and other citizens across wide social, political, and economic spectra.

There is a strong sense in which educational projections, programs, and leadership must relate to reality and humanity. To see the import of cognitive, affective, and psychomotor developments as basic emphases in educational designs requires a realistic consideration of the human condition. Education is for people, and the smallest abstract conception must be humanized in order to give it a sense of cogency, both in time and place.

Humanizing the educational process becomes a response to the question of tempering feelings with reality. When Lomita Fundamental School, a "magnet" school in California, shuns "social promotions" and, instead, incorporates an educational plan that sets goals, stresses academics and discipline, and encourages cooperation among educators, parents, and students, it is taking a realistic and humanistic approach to education and life. Thus, instead of promoting students primarily on the premises of "feelings," schools should assume an honest and realistic posture. They should identify and assess the problems which inhibit educational growth and development and, using this assessment, restructure educational programs and strategies that enable students to reach established goals.

A humanistic approach to education and life implies that those who undertake the educative task should do so from a professional as well as a moral frame of reference. Professionally, it means teaching with expertise,

---

[30] James Lipham and James Hoeh, Jr., *The Principalship: Foundations and Functions* (New York: Harper and Row, 1974), p. 5.

spirit, and a sense of accountability to challenge and motivate students to work to their fullest capacity. Morally, it means demonstrating an honesty of purpose and action that carries a conviction that realistic preparation is necessary for enabling students to enter the adult world as viable citizens with requisite skills for assuming the rights and obligations which citizenship demands.

The conceptualization and effectuation of these critical concerns help to create an environment of trust and safety. Such an environment provides a climate in which youngsters learn to cope with societal trends by living within a set of rules and laws in society, knowing what is expected of them, learning to think before they act, and learning to fulfill those expectations.[31]

Schools can make a difference in the mental, social, physical, and academic competence of children. When educational leaders believe in what they are doing, they achieve success. They work because they subscribe to the program. With cooperation, parents, too, can become involved in the reinforcement of the school's educational goals. The net result is a flourish of freshness, will, and zest.

The importance of George Counts' classic challenge articulated in his work, *Dare the School Build a New Social Order?*, is very cogent today, given the sweep of the prevailing "new pessimism" in education. Our public schools are not obsolete and ineffectual.

Schools can choose to promote or squelch the socialization process. They have largely chosen to ignore many of their critical functions to society's detriment—a detriment that can be measured in terms of the harsh realities of the social conditions and resultant behavior patterns of some citizens. There must be a new thrust to turn things around, to upgrade prevailing circumstances. Education en masse is expensive, but children are priceless, and the neglect of their education becomes a dangerous risk.

Teachers do not necessarily have to "love" their students in order to teach well. They ought, however, to respect them, to care for them, to discipline them, and to keep them in school. Above all, they have a moral, professional, and paid responsibility to teach all children. It is their responsibility to be accountable. Good educational leadership demands it.

Public schools cannot continue to miseducate segments of their citizenry without ensuring the nation's demise in the long run. A chain is as strong as its weakest links; therefore, the link of an uneducated mass sets the tone for a volatile situation.

A viable taxpayer is an asset to a state's fiscal health. Any mechanism which short-circuits efforts to educate or interferes with developing poten-

---

[31] David Mutch, "The Challenge to Excellence," *American Educator* 2 (Winter 1978): 20-22, 52-53.

tial, serves only deleterious ends. The short-changing of middle-class children, reflected in the dramatic drop in aptitude test scores,[32] is an area of general concern which no longer can be rationalized through the spurious excuse of blaming school failures on bad communities, dumb parents, a lack of books in homes, or children who do not want to learn. As Glasser suggests, this is a sad rationalization that too many educators embrace.

Close examination of the case studies shows a certain consistency at work throughout these success-oriented models. Organizationally, the programs have set goals that are well defined and actualized. This critical factor enables the participants to make progress and measure it. Their philosophies of education and program rationale engender respect, courtesy, and high moral standards within highly disciplined environments. Parents are involved in the reinforcement of educational goals, and teachers work because they subscribe to the programs. When teachers believe in what they are doing, there is usually success.

Whether the program is in rural Vermont, suburban Cincinnati, or metro-core Southern California, the curriculum, administrative, and teaching arrangements of group work, open education, and modular or flexible scheduling reflect a high sense of motivation among students, parents, and educational leaders. Students are more likely to be motivated when they have some choice in the flexibility that is required to attain success.

Success generates success and invites full expressiveness in the nurturing of specific theoretical givens, unique talents, and attributes of students who differ in all sorts of ways from one another.

Models of Essentials for Educational Leadership

Educational problems are complex in nature and national in scope. School failure is pervasive and so is success. Paramount to all educational success, whether minimal or grandiose, is the leadership which sets the pace and administrates the district, the school, and the programs.

Educational leadership admits no simplistic remedies. However, the public expects and demands them. It looks for remedies in the form of productivity. Since the problems usually identified by the media are symptoms of major, complex problems, educational leadership needs to address and then translate the philosophies and theories that underlie the best available knowledge about education.

Unfortunately, problems affecting educational leadership are stuck in the mire of controversies such as methods vs. content, emotional develop-

[32] William Glasser, "Disorders in Our Schools: Causes and Remedies," *Phi Delta Kappan* 59 (January 1978): 331-333.

ment vs. intellectual growth, basic skills vs. the whole child, and so on. Educational leadership should not be expected to thrive within the confines of such rigid dichotomous relationships; its scope should transcend these and other limits. Leadership change should be systematically accomplished in collaboration with students, parents, experienced and knowledgeable teachers, and significant others.

Democratic leadership must have as its basis freedom and added responsibility. Freedom implies available options and respect for individuals and groups. Responsibility should incorporate support for the development of self-direction, shared obligations, and the insurance of a quality education. Democratic leadership must facilitate action which transcends heightened awareness.

Educational leadership must emerge out of programs which bring educational leaders into broader community involvement, thereby penetrating issues of common concerns. This may be done by using simulations and making face-to-face contact with business people and those associated with city resources, such as labor unions, social, political, economic, and community agencies. The process may also include the analysis of the legislative process, the media, and other viable extensions of both private and public sectors.

The outcome should develop closer relationships between communities and schools. Such relationships can lead to several types of educational benefits. Schools can provide substantive background and content knowledge; they can set the stage for developing the processes and skills of decision-making and systems management. The communities can provide arenas for learning about people and problems in our pluralistic society. Knowledge thus gained can facilitate practice in problem-solving by addressing issues affecting the education of the young. Educational leaders must confront and find solutions for dichotomous views on differing values and philosophies.

Educational leadership requires the acceptance of responsibility for exercising strong and constructive influences on American education. It requires the same responsibility for progress, advocating reforms, and engaging others as collaborative participants working towards positive change, democratic and humanistic ideals, moral values, and changing human conditions in an evolving world.

Educational leaders must continue to be aware of and sensitive to critical issues, and willing to translate this awareness and sensitivity into participatory action. They must proceed to point the way by first addressing their own particular needs through training and retraining and by coming to terms with criticism and requests for accountability. Educational leaders must utilize time, energy, and resources with cost-productive efficiency;

identify needs; set and prioritize goals; and translate these goals with moral and professional authority.

Educational leadership should assume the structure of a system which provides a new type of training for all participants who are involved in the teaching-learning process. In essence, positive educational leadership must be identified with strategies which make desirable changes a continuous process rather than a periodic and traumatic alteration of artificial standards. The continuous process must also be infused with a spirit that encourages the development and use of new and improved practices, as well as the formulation of desirable organizational, structural, and financial change.

Finally, urban educational leadership must assume bold, dynamic foresight in its mission, a spirit of determination in its commitment, and a capacity and preparedness which are indicative of quality. It must buttress these conditions by capitalizing on the selectivity of unique possibilities found in the larger urban environment. Thus, urban educational leadership must seize the opportunity to enable people to adjust to and enjoy the ambiance of urban life and to orient them to future life planning.

School personnel can transcend the confines of their immediate social system. Through the incorporation of the principle of democratic social participation, they can expose to wider view the complexity of school problems and thereby unite the larger community in efforts to resolve the educational problems which affect everyone in the social structure. Social participation should mean the application of knowledge, thought, expertise, and commitment in the educational arena, at various levels.

Urban educational leadership, especially in a pluralistic and free society, demands reaching out to others in the public and private sectors of the urban communities. The outcome of collaborative efforts can result in constructive interaction between school systems and the public-private sectors, the provision of opportunities for sharing ideas, and the promulgation of action which benefits the nation's health.

3
Developing Curriculum in an Urban Context

H. Prentice Baptiste, Jr., and James E. Anderson

Because of various conditions existing in the urban environments of our society (such as overcrowding, inadequate lifespace, low incomes, high unemployment, ethnic and racial discrimination, declining tax bases, and numerous other factors), most of the traditional educational processes and curricula have been rendered ineffective by the tenacity of the urban press.[1] As one closely observes the educational processes, particularly the irrelevance of curricula in many urban schools, it is neither difficult nor profound to realize that urban realities and conditions are giving schools their most severe tests. Unfortunately, as a result, many urban schools have greatly failed in their role to responsibly educate their students to deal with the realities of life.

The failure of urban schools to address the realities of urban environments has added to the growing negativism and alienation which is engulfing many cities. Coupled with the nature of the urban press and poverty of the urban spirit, these conditions have taken a devastating toll on both young and old. The sheer immensity and complexity of the physical and psychological problems indigenous to many of these areas have stifled and often suffocated all motivations for improvement and change.

An Analysis of the Determinants of Curriculum in an Urban Environment

The United States has recently witnessed the emergence of a generation of individuals, particularly children, who have adopted significantly unique lifestyles. These lifestyles, which include the development of various value systems and behaviors, reflect a set of cultural experiences

---

[1] Susan Cahill and M. F. Cooper, eds., *The Urban Reader* (Englewood Cliffs, N.J.: Prentice Hall, 1972), p. 416.

basically different from those anticipated by the traditional educational system. What is needed is an educational system and, specifically, a curriculum that focus on the basic determinants of curricular-societal needs, student needs, and content *from an urban perspective*. Due to the enormity of this task and the unlimited possible alternatives or solutions to these problems, this analysis has been limited to the basic determinants of curriculum. The notion of traditionalism, viewing various tasks in educational development and change through traditional frames of reference, has hindered our effectiveness to bring about significant new dimensions in educational institutions. Regarding the nature of the urban environment, the working frame of reference is in close accord with that of Fantini, who emphasizes that "the urban context is one in which there is a persistent stress imposed by intensely concentrated realities."[2]

The urban cultural crucible contains unique ethnic, racial and socio-economic continuums which, combined, create urban dynamics identifiable in most of our large cities. Simultaneously, however, if anything is known about societal dynamics, it is that values, problems, ideas, and trends do not stop with our urban areas; they are encountered in many types of living environments.[3]

Societal Needs

Schools and curricula should not attempt to serve as social controls. No longer can the curriculum labor toward this insidious goal. Within the historical purpose of education, to provide social control, pupils were taught to be punctual, diligent, and to have respect for material success and their betters. Schools were not concerned with the development of intellectual capabilities but rather with the processing of raw human material into the harmony of an orderly capitalistic society.[4]

In meeting the needs of society, the urban community has been forced to ignore its own needs and pressures. Many writers have indicated that the purpose of curriculum is to maintain a stable society by emphasizing specified knowledges, skills, values, and sentiments. Subsequently, the curriculum transmitted those cultural roots considered significant and im-

[2] Mario Fantini and Gerald Weinstein, *Making Urban Schools Work: Social Realities and the Urban School* (New York: Holt, Reinhart and Winston, Inc., 1968), p. 3.

[3] Richard Wisniewski, ed., *Teaching About Life in the City*, in *1972 Yearbook of the National Council for the Social Studies* (Washington, D.C.: National Council for the Social Studies, 1972), p. 3.

[4] James Richardson, "The Historical Roots of Our Urban Crises," *Conflict and Change in Education,* ed. Francis Lanni (Glenview: Scott, Foresman and Company, 1975), p. 343.

portant by the controlling facets of the larger society. Thus the curriculum is interwoven with the social fabric that sustains it. Curriculum as a major component of education is concerned with the problem of maintaining the society as a closely knit and well-integrated unit. The major function of curriculum has been to maintain the society status quo.

As Smith, Stanley, and Shores point out, the fabric of a curriculum is derived from those fundamental universals (that is, values, sentiments, knowledges, skills) that provide society with stability and vitality and individuals with the motivations and controls of conduct.[5] All knowledge is socially distributed and the selection of the knowledge to be distributed, as Sizemore so aptly puts it, is made by the controlling cultural groups of any society.[6] The most important aspects of the curriculum deal with the values and standards for maintaining an open–class society. The basic political and economic theories and practices which logically would be more important for enhancing an open–class society unjustly remain of secondary importance in the curriculum. As Sizemore has indicated, the paradigm for our capitalistic system is purposely not taught in our schools.[7]

Smith recognizes three basic societies: (a) homogeneous, (b) heterogeneous, and (c) plural.[8] In the rare homogeneous society, all groups within a political unit share the same total institutional system. In the heterogeneous society, such as the United States, all groups share the same basic institutions while simultaneously participating in alternative and exclusive institutions. The plural society differs from the others in that groups in the same political unit do not share basic institutions. Thus each group has its own distinctive religious, educational, and economic institutions. Pacheo states that alternative institutions are those in which members of groups can freely elect to participate, while exclusive institutions are limited in membership to those who belong to clearly defined groups.[9] Dickeman stated that American society reflects the characteristics of a caste society more than of an open–class society.[10] If this is true, then the societal demands of a heterogeneous society are biasly differentiated. This is supported by Smith, Stanley and Shores:

[5] B. Othanel Smith, William O. Stanley, and S. Harlan Shores, *Fundamentals of Curriculum Development* (New York: Harcourt, Brace, and World, Inc., 1957), p. 8.
[6] Barbara Sizemore, "Power Inclusion Model," South Bend, Ind., 1970 (videotaped).
[7] Ibid.
[8] M. G. Smith, *The Plural Society in the British West Indies* (Berkeley: University of California Press, 1971).
[9] Arturo Pacheo, "Cultural Pluralism: A Philosophical Analysis," *Journal of Teacher Education* 28 (May-June 1977): 8.
[10] Mildred Dickeman, "Multicultural Education: An Anthropological Perspective." Keynote Address at the ASCD National Curriculum Study Institute on Multicultural Education, New Orleans, April 1977.

The point of this discussion is not that all vocational education is class education. Only in societies where certain vocations are associated with particular social classes will this tend to be true. Social systems that emphasize an open-door policy for all occupations—making it possible for every individual irrespective of race, creed, or social background to acquire the knowledges and skills he is capable and desirous of obtaining—will reduce the charges that some occupations will be monopolized by privileged classes. In these societies vocational education will be least associated with class education.[11]

They also point out that class education is sometimes confused with common education.[12] Thus the societal demands of a heterogeneous society may be insidious for some of its clientele.

Any proposed curriculum for urban students must challenge the caste-status character of societal demands. The curriculum for urban schools must not be a passive vessel for maintaining the status quo. It must become the active force for transforming this society and meeting the needs of the students it serves—to transform the culture, not to perpetuate it. It must receive both its intrinsic and extrinsic power from its urban clientele who, however, must realize that they are constantly in a power struggle for control of the curriculum. One may represent this power relationship as A/B whereas A represents a group with power and B represents a group with no power. It is our contention that the urban community is a group without power. This group (that is, B group, urban clientele) urgently needs to control the urban curriculum if it desires its students to be successful and not just to fulfill the lower level of our heterogeneous societal demands.

The process of education is not neutral. Urban education will either function as a process for integrating urban youth into the logic of the present system and bring about conformity to it or, as Schuall points out, it may serve as a freeing process as urban residents discover how to deal critically and creatively with changes in their environment.[13] These changes will occur only if the urban community attains a position of power and control over its own environment.

All curricula contain forms of hidden societal controls that are usually not deliberate and may be very subtle. For example, myths and values exert an influence over societal control, as do forms of child rearing. As Bruner wrote in 1966: "This aspect of control is often referred to by anthropologists as covert culture."[14] That is, the real controls or controlling

[11] Smith, Stanley, and Shores, p. 8.
[12] Ibid.
[13] Richard Schaull, Forward to *Pedagogy of the Oppressed,* by Paulo Freire (New York: Herder and Herder, 1971), p. 15.
[14] Jerome Bruner, *On Knowing: Essay for the Left Hand* (New York: Atheneum, 1966), p. 131.

values are concealed under a false shield of freedom. Bruner further states:

> There are two approaches to the problem of control. One of them, the one that is least often a target for moral indignation, consists in seeking to control men by shaping their conception of the world in which they live. Once we have determined how men shall perceive and structure the world with which they have commerce, we can safely leave their actions to them in the sense that, if they believe themselves to be standing before a precipice they will not step over it unless they intend suicide. This is cognitive control, controlling men's minds. Achieving such control is exceedingly difficult or rather, usurping it is difficult, for the control now rests in the culture and its way of introducing members into its web of reality.[15]

The implications of the control of urban curriculum by any societal group except the urban clientele is utterly clear from the preceding statement. Tantamount to the survival and productivity of an urban community is the evolvement of its control over the school curricula, which will fulfill the real need of its youth.

Content and Values

Many educators erroneously behave as though content were synonymous with curriculum. Furthermore, it is assumed that *all* content must come from the disciplines.[16] This, too, is a false assumption for any curriculum and especially for curriculum in urban schools.

Contrary to Phenix,[17] nondisciplined knowledge is suitable for teaching and learning. A great proportion of the primary content should evolve from the student's life experiences, "real" problems and projects, and should be appropriately supplemented with content from the disciplines. Urban curriculum developers can no longer allow the disciplines to follow their traditional role of setting the pattern for the curriculum.

If we accept the premise that all education is value-laden and that the curriculum is the vehicle for delivering education, then the curriculum is value-laden, normative, and tends to create and sustain a certain set of beliefs, customs, attitudes, and institutions.[18]

[15] Ibid.
[16] Philip Phenix, "The Use of the Disciplines as Curriculum Content," *The Subjects in the Curriculum,* ed. Frank L. Steeves (New York: The Odyssey Press, 1968), pp. 1-10.
[17] Ibid.
[18] James Banks, "Curricular Models for an Open Society," *Education for an Open Society,* eds. Delmo Della-Dora and James E. House (Washington, D.C.: Association for Supervision and Curriculum Development, 1974), p. 43.

What values will the curriculum embellish for the urban student? Curriculum developers and other urban educators have failed to realize the significance and importance of this question.

Values are those intangibles which are held in high esteem by most members of society, which permeate the core of societal institutions, and which are translated into norms and customs to thus serve as controls of human conduct. Within a heterogeneous society values can have a differentiating effect on inhabitants—that is, not all inhabitants can or will be allowed to exhibit the values to the same degree. In actuality some values benefit some societal members yet penalize others. An example of such a value is racism. The differentiating effect of this value should be obvious. Nevertheless, all members are enculturated to place a high esteem on all societal values, regardless of the effect of those values. Values deemed detrimental to urban peoples should be eliminated from the urban curriculum, and the values considered important should be incorporated into the curriculum. The latter are categorized as social action values, cultural values, and pedagogic values.

Social Action Values. An urban curriculum must generate constructive and effective social advocates. The values of such a curriculum must be charged with an essence of group liberation, group solidarity, and potential group power. Urban students should have a thorough knowledge of our political system and a perspective of its reality from their powerless position in a caste society. A high value should be placed on problem-solving strategies which utilize data from the students' environment. Banks and Sizemore have advocated the importance of curriculum programs imparting to urban students the significance of power along with effective strategies for attaining it. In order for these power models to be effective, a new set of values must be accepted. Individual competition must be supplemented with strategies for group cohesion and cooperation. Individual power must be replaced by emphasis on group power and nationalistic belief in the humanity of one's own group.

Cultural Values. The relevance of a group's culture to its success in education has been expounded on by a number of multicultural education scholars.[19] The significance of this relevance is proportional to the extent the group's culture is included in a positive manner within the curriculum. Banks argues eloquently in his discussion of the alien school culture.

[19] James Banks, "Cultural Pluralism and the Schools," *Educational Leadership* 32 (December 1974): 164.

Many ethnic minority youths find the school culture alien, hostile, and self-defeating. Because of institutional racism, poverty, and other complex factors, most ethnic minority communities are characterized by numerous values, institutions, behavior patterns, and linguistic traits which differ in significant ways from the dominant society. The youths who are socialized within these ethnic communities enter the school with cultural characteristics which the school rejects and demeans. These youths are also dehumanized in the school because they are non-white. Because of the negative ways in which their cultural and racial traits are viewed by the school, educators fail to help most minority youths to acquire the skills which they need to function effectively within the two cultural worlds in which they must survive. Consequently, many of them drop out of school, psychologically and physically.

Urban curriculum programs must endeavor to teach those cultural values which will render curricula most effective. Certainly, the curriculum cannot draw from the general society those oppressive values, such as racism, which tend to dehumanize certain members of society. The urban curriculum has a double function. It must aggressively strive to cancel or eradicate the harmful effects of the general society's cultural values—for example, maleness, white/European ancestry, and money—on its clientele.[20] At the same time the urban curriculum must aggressively incorporate those values which will make it most effective. This effectiveness must be measured by the extent to which urban students become independent, self-actualizing learners.

Pedagogic Values. A deterence to the success of any urban curriculum lies in its support of certain pedagogic values. To avoid a merely cosmetic curriculum change, the roles of teachers and students must be radically changed. Furthermore, the role of the community must become more substantial in the pedagogic processes of the curriculum.

A dialogic process involving both teacher and student as pursuers of knowledge relevant to the conditions of the urban environment must undergird the urban curriculum. Paulo Freire expresses the nature of this dialogic process: "Authentic education is not carried on by 'A' for 'B' or by 'A' about 'B', but rather by 'A' with 'B' mediated by the world—a world which impresses and challenges both parties, giving rise to views or opinions about it."[21]

Therefore, the essence of urban interaction is dialogue. Instead of a hierarchical relationship among its administrators, teachers, students, and community members, there must exist an equalitarian relationship. Hier-

[20] Sizemore, "Power Inclusion Model."
[21] Paulo Freire, *Pedagogy of the Oppressed* (New York: Herder and Herder, 1971), p. 82.

archical decision-making models impede communication in the dialogic processes of the urban curriculum.[22]

Curriculum development processes, particularly those focusing on urban schools, must be more dialogic in concept and more equalitarian in nature. Urban curriculum is more congruent with the interactive position of Smith, Stanley, and Shores.[23] Students' needs must be viewed prismatically through their culture and immediate environment. The urban culture must be recognized and utilized to its fullest. Ignoring the characteristics of the urban culture is as tantamount to the failure of a curriculum program for urban students as the lack of inclusion of the middle–class culture would be for suburban schools. The cultural elements of the urban community form a pattern which judiciously links itself to the soul of the urban child. It is not enough for curriculum developers to recognize this cultural pattern. It must be analyzed and translated into an effective component of all urban curricula.

This discussion of urban curriculum development focuses on several questions. What are some functional goals and objectives for specific urban curriculum in the area of general goal directives and objectives? What kind of curricula design could effectively encompass these functional goals and objectives and provide a curricular "frame of reference" from which meaningful learning experiences can be developed? What would be the learning products for the students from a curriculum designed with this perspective? What are some examples of learning experiences and urban curricular programs that have delivered learning products that reflect urban curriculum goals and objectives? What are some suggested processes for facilitating this type of urban curriculum development?

Functional Goals and Objectives for the Urban Curriculum

In order to facilitate optimum learning experiences with goals designed for students who live in urban areas, the curriculum must represent the cultural context of urban reality. The challenge for meaningful urban curriculum building emerges in greater clarity. Directly related to the development of significant learning experiences is the development of multifunctional goals to provide the knowledge, skills, and behaviors necessary for students in urban settings. The process of selecting and developing

[22] Barbara Sizemore, "Shattering the Melting Pot Myth," *Teaching Ethnic Studies,* ed. James Banks (Washington, D.C.: National Council for the Social Studies, 1973), p. 87.

[23] Smith, Stanley, and Shores, p. 8.

those goals is neither simple nor quick, but one in which the urban student's reality and social action, cultural and pedagogic values become the philosophical point of departure for curriculum planning and development.

From the standpoint of urban curriculum development, selected goals must assist urban students in coping with urban culture and life experiences and provide expansive cross-cultural learning dimensions at the same time. The further significance of this action is that instead of attempting to gain abstractions of knowledge for "cognitive stockpiling," the emphasis would be on developing a group of life skills that would enable students to become more self-determining, with higher levels of commitment to human dignity. Additionally, this curriculum would be directed to a greater recognition and respect for human diversity built around moral-personal attitude skills that will enable students to participate positively and efficiently in their own environment. Secondly, it could provide them with cross-cultural universals that would allow them to operate successfully in environments outside of their own.

The development of skills as a means of becoming more powerful and self-determining and as the primary focus for learning experiences in urban environments offers two immediate suggestions. First, the complexities and conditions of urban environments have left students lacking in critical knowledge and meaningful skills to make themselves operative in their environments. Second, any significant change in curricula for urban context will need to assist students in acquiring those skills and needed knowledge. It is clear that the quality of life for people in urban areas is not improved by describing what their existence is like or how it should be, but by working with urban residents in seeking a better life for us all.[24]

Various research studies have pointed out that in urban environments the need to be able to control one's actions and interactions, both at the individual and group levels as well as at the institutional level, is a primary need, and thus should be an ultimate goal. The specification of skill and knowledge development for urban school students is a significant part of the curriculum development process and primarily an analytically deductive procedure that can be illustrated in the following way:

From

Exemplars of Goal Directives for Curricula in Urban School Environments

Self-Determination—Self-Actualization
Commitment to Human Dignity and Humanity

[24] Wisniewski, p. 10.

Recognition and Respect for Human Diversity
Intrinsic Cognitive—Affective Preparation
Equilibrated Moral—Attitude and Ethnic Topology

To

Exemplars of General Objectives for Curricula in Urban School Environments

The curriculum in urban school environments must facilitate student learning in the areas of self-discovery, self-awareness, self-identity and self-development.

The curriculum in urban school environments must facilitate student learning in becoming more knowledgeable of urban environments.

The curriculum in urban school environments must facilitate student learning in basic skills.

The curriculum in urban school environments must facilitate student learning in the development of respect for human diversity.

The curriculum in urban school environments must facilitate student learning in the development of problem–solving skills.

The curriculum in urban school environments must facilitate student learning in the development of social action skills to change and influence the community, environment, or societal reality of urban areas.

The curriculum in urban school environments must facilitate student learning in the identification and development of occupational and career development perspectives.

The urban school environment in America today demands curricular learning experiences that can provide multiple learning products. Moving from the nature of curriculum goal directives for urban education to general objectives to specified skill and knowledge development clusters, it is evident that the process of identifying skill development areas is important. Individuals' inhumanity to others, the nature of urban pressures, and the loss of a positive and productive "urban spirit" are all indicative of the psychological and intellectual tasks that face urban schools. It is mandatory that students obtain behaviors and skills to help them survive, cope, and become productive. The "internal notion" of curriculum in American education has been an academic proclivity for knowledge acquisition in traditional learning environments. However, with the unique "heteromix" of ethnic, racial, and socio-economic groups combining to bring about diversified lifestyles and different value systems, the need for relevant education has become serious.

Over the past few years, several educators and those being educated have indicated that there is a need to provide "life skills" as well as "life knowledge."[25] People have talked about different kinds of skills that curricula in general could deliver in various ways. Meade identifies the most needed skills as the ability to exploit one's personal creativity in responding to life and in the use of leisure time, and the ability to retain one's individuality and autonomy within the larger group.[26] Fantini and Weinstein feel that, along with such "academic skills" as the ability to compute, read, and outline, students in urban environments need skills in self-awareness, negotiating with adults, and organizing people for change.[27] Additionally, clusters such as language arts have been proposed to include such skills as locating information, organizing information, and communicating orally and in writing. Numerous others have also been described by Joyce and Banks as being relevant for culturally diverse populations.[28]

Nevertheless, the current curricula designs in most urban schools still remain virtually chained to what Baker, Browdy, Beecher and Ho call the subject matter centered design.[29] This design pursues the mastery of subject matter rather than cognitive life skills for urban environments or promotion of affective behavior development necessary for metropolitan areas.

Other general curricular design patterns have tried to either correlate or develop different configurations and have also, generally, been ineffective in providing urban life skills.

The begging questions then become obvious. "What are the more effective curricula designs and what kinds of learning experiences are most desired?" The answers to these questions in the past have primarily represented frames of reference, value systems, goals, objectives, subject matter, and instructional methodologies that reflect the interests of people other than those who live in urban environments. Similarly, future decisions concerning urban schooling, and curricula in particular, will have to be

[25] Louis Rubin, ed., *Life Skills in School and Society* (Washington, D.C.: Association for Supervision and Curriculum Development, 1969).

[26] Edward J. Meade, "The Changing Society and Its Schools," *Life Skills in Schools and Society,* ed. Louis Rubin (Washington, D.C.: Association for Supervision and Curriculum Development, 1969), p. 51.

[27] Fantini and Weinstein, pp. 25-31.

[28] William Joyce and James Banks, eds., *Teaching the Language Arts to Culturally Different Children* (Reading, Mass.: Addison-Wesley, 1971).

[29] Gwendolyn C. Baker, Marshall Browdy, Clarence Beecher, and Robert Ho, "Modifying Curriculums to Meet Multicultural Needs," *Teaching in a Multicultural Society,* eds. Delores E. Cross, Gwendolyn C. Baker, and Lindheg J. Stiles (New York: Free Press, 1977), p. 146.

made by people who are interested in those living in urban areas, and using the dialogic processes previously discussed.

In terms of processes for developing more effective urban curricula, the exact configuration of the designs will probably take shape and become functional as the specific urban community demands. However, effective curricula designs for urban schools will, in most cases, contain a cadre of centralizing components that will be facilitative for urban learning environments.

The most important fact of the curriculum design issue is, without a doubt, the frame of reference from which the learning experience will be derived, Baker, Browdy, Beecher, and Ho refer to this type of curriculum design as the "persistent life situation." [30] In this curriculum, goals and objectives directly relate to the kinds of experiences, responsibilities, and needs that the student must face in his daily living environment; learning is focused on skills, concepts, thought processes, and information that will help young people solve problems and function effectively in life situations. We offer here some suggested combinations of specific skill and knowledge development clusters that would provide relevant learning products for students in pressure-filled urban areas.

Exemplars of Specific Skill and Knowledge Development Clusters for Curriculum in Urban School Environments

Self-Actualization—Interpersonal Skills

Basic Skills

Communication Skills

Problem Solving—Decision-Making and Social Action Skills

Occupational—Career Identity Awareness and Development Skills

The essence of the urban methodology is dialogue and it is upon this premise that the ultimate dynamics of a curriculum development process must proceed. With this idea as a philosophical cornerstone to build upon, one of the most significant challenges for the urban educator is the planning and organization of a process for accomplishing this task.

Process to Assist in the Development of New Curriculum Dimensions for Urban Settings

PART I.

Question 1. How can an urban curriculum development process begin?

Question 2. Who should serve on an urban curriculum task force?

---

[30] Ibid, p. 147.

Initially the process might begin with the creation of an urban curriculum task force, a working group of concerned individuals who could lead in the planning and development of the curriculum products. This interim task force, which could be convened by a school district administrator, principal, faculty member, parent, community person, or even a student at the secondary level, would have the responsibilities of cloistering other concerned individuals and representatives of various groups for data gathering and initial input into the planning phase.

The task force could work during the regular school year or through the summer. This working group might include selected individuals such as knowledgeable school faculty, community representatives, students, parents, local school district personnel, curriculum specialists, subject matter or content specialists, selected special interest groups such as local businessmen, community service organization representatives, municipal government officials, and grassroots organizations. During the time specified, the task force and its sub-groups could be assigned to respond to various questions and begin working on various tasks.

Question 3. How can one develop an urban curriculum task force into a cohesive, directed, highly diversified, and effective working group?

Step 1. Engage the task force members in introspective and self-assessment experiences to examine their own values, philosophies, personal frames of reference, predispositions, biases, opinions, and prejudices as they relate to education in urban schools and settings.

Step 2. Engage the task force members in exploring new and different knowledge bases and experiences as they relate to expanding their understanding of urban environments and education in those environments.

Step 3. Initiate and develop meaningful dialectic processes among task force members and with school personnel, parents, students, community people, businesses, and government representatives, about all facets of education in urban environments. (Use divergencies in opinions and viewpoints as strengths of the task force and prepare the group for compromise and negotiation in subsequent decision-making.)

Step 4. Identify and interpret the specific curriculum problems in the urban education environment on which the task force should focus, and examine their relationship to previous curriculum goals, objectives, practices, outcomes, student and societal needs, racial and ethnic group needs and experiences, and curriculum materials that have or have not been in use.

Step 5. Interpret and organize the dialogues, experiences, and data collected into task force general statements of positions and philosophies as they relate to urban (a) curriculum goals, objectives, and skills; (b) student learning outcomes; (c) nature of instructional strategies and learning experiences for urban educational settings; and (d) use of the urban environment in the urban educational experience.[31]

Thus, the task force should be reflective of all of the sectors of the community. Its total effectiveness will ultimately be directly accountable to those sectors.

PART II.

Question 1. What are some of the initial roles and tasks that an urban curriculum task force and its sub-task groups or committees can perform?

Step 1. Develop work channels and communication lines with all projected groups that might be involved in the curriculum development project, including school district administrative and supervisory personnel, school boards, community groups, students, parents, and classroom teachers concerning needs, instructional innovations, and critical educational issues that are confronting the urban communities.

Step 2. Review available research and related literature on curriculum development strategies and how they relate to education in urban environments, particularly in the areas of goals, objectives and skills, general decisions about curriculum and instruction strategies, use of curriculum resources, nature of learning, roles of the teacher and the student, purpose of the content, and the nature of evaluation processes. (These components must be studied from urban-focused perspectives and the aforementioned general statements of philosophy of the urban curriculum task force.)

Step 3. Initiate an identification and selection process for individuals who will actually serve or be a part of the curriculum development tasks and identify the specific directions in which the project will move. It will be their task to see that the project stays on target to meet the needs of all the urban demographical groups which these schools serve. (Needs assessment and/or delineation of projected student roles offer two conceptualizations for approaching these tasks (Archiniega and Mazon, 1974).)

---

[31] James Anderson, "Critical Perspectives on the Development of Multicultural Teacher Education," Research and development paper (University of Houston, 1977), pp. 18-19. The format and content of the five tasks represent a partial adaptive synthesis of the ways in which curriculum leadership groups may assist in curriculum development, as presented in the paper.

As the curriculum task force moves through some of the initial planning, organizational, and early developmental roles, it is likely to become more apparent that the dynamics of this kind of curriculum development process are, at least, two-dimensional. The "substantive" dimension consists of new curriculum content ideas and philosophies and the "procedural" dimension consists of developing and progressing through a sequentially oriented process to complete the project. Each has a separate but interlocking identity.

In the substantive sense, the "persistent life situations" curriculum design focuses on skills, concepts, thought processes, and information that will help young people solve problems and function more effectively in their life situations. It is this type of curriculum design in an urban-focused sense, integrating skill and knowledge development clusters, that can provide new learning dimensions. Within this type of curriculum focus, the skills component can offer great potential for educational impact and student development. Additionally, the need to provide learning experiences which develop and promote affective and cognitive dimensions is of the highest priority, as is the development of active stances in learning. Thus, using the previously stated goals, directives, and general objectives as needed entities for new urban curriculum development processes, important questions emerge in the substantive sense.

Question 2. What are some of the specific skill knowledge cluster concepts that could be utilized as points of departure for new types of learning?

Question 3. How can a city or urban area with its variety of resources become a part of the curriculum in a planned learning environment?

In order to respond to these questions, a short examination of each of the skill and knowledge areas is helpful.

Self-Actualization and Interpersonal Skills

The urban environment has been a psychological testing ground for the interfacing of technology and industrialization with social traditions, values, and humanity. Students find themselves in the midst of changing urban cultural contexts in which, as Johnson points out, values are changing from a nondirected, achievement-oriented puritanical emphasis to a self-actualizing emphasis, stressing development of personal resources, the experiencing of joy, and a sense of fulfillment in one's life.[32] It is in this

---

[32] David W. Johnson, *Reaching Out: Interpersonal Effectiveness and Self-Actualization* (Englewood Cliffs, N.J.: Prentice Hall, 1972), p. 2.

direction that urban curriculum must take some giant strides. The process for student self-actualization in today's urban environment must consciously tie the past and the future to the present in meaningful continuity while assisting the student in living up to his or her fullest capacity. It is important that curriculum experiences counteract urban pressures, assist students in developing their self-potential, and help them tie that potential to self-developed working goals.

In no way are we advocating doing away with the idea of achievement or replacing it with other ideas. Rather, achievement goes hand-in-hand with self-actualization; their goals and directions are not only interactive but interdependent and, thus, cannot be treated in isolation from one another.

The development of interpersonal skills with the planned curriculum becomes the foundation for the self-actualization process [33] in the following areas: (1) knowing and trusting each other, (2) accurately and clearly understanding each other, (3) influencing and helping each other, and (4) constructively resolving problems and conflicts in relationships with others.

New York's Bank Street College of Education has established parent-child development centers in school districts in Detroit, New Orleans, Houston, Indianapolis, and San Antonio that provide learning experiences for mothers and children in social development and interpersonal skills. Programs such as Project GRASP in Philadelphia, which was designed to work with high–achieving children in the second grade, placed emphasis on growth, response, achievement, self-esteem, and participation, and used thematic approaches that made use of learning resources, including skill-building field trips and creative dramatics.[34]

The five-year project at Cleveland High in Seattle, Washington, has been directed toward working with "disruptive youths." Incorporated into the conscience of the school was a climate of trust, caring, and mutual respect for students. The project staff treated the students as individuals. The curriculum involved students in effective communication, problem-solving, and decision-making processes that fostered self-actualization and the development of the students as responsible persons.[35]

Schools in Madison, Wisconsin, have also successfully utilized curriculum in the human relations area. Curriculum development efforts in the "Dialogue-Inquiry" Approach deals with intergrating and coordinating

---

[33] Ibid., p. 3.

[34] I. Ezra Staples, "Affecting Disaffected Students: The Philadelphia Story," *Educational Leadership* 34 (1977): 424.

[35] William Maynard, "Working with Disruptive Youth," *Educational Leadership* 34 (1977): 417.

ideas and feelings so that interactions among people have purpose and are productive. The "Individual Differences" Approach deals with attitudes of students toward differences in the "human family."

Another unique project with a much broader scope that made use of community resources in the 1960's and 1970's was the Roberson Center for Arts and Sciences in Binghamton, New York, which demonstrated how to move community resources in the arts, history, and sciences into the schools.[36] This program provided learning experiences for pre-schoolers through adults in art, music, movement, visual arts, crafts, theater, dance history, and science, with emphasis on self-actualization and self-interest. Its goal was to offer students opportunities for personal experiences and involvement with the realities of human expression, understanding, and knowledge. During a three-year period, over 760,000 students were involved with such community resources as astronomical societies, fine arts societies, garden centers, historical societies, performing arts groups, museums, mobil business programs, hospitals, city government, and local industries.

Basic Skills. Basic skills involve literacy skills that allow students to achieve a functional literacy.[37] In the urban environment, the question of "fundamentals or basics," as some refer to it, is mute. Regardless of the environment, the abilities to read, write, speak, compute, and develop psychomotor skills have always been of primary importance.

The main concerns in this area have been the instructional and cultural contexts in which teachers and educators have attempted to deliver these skills. In urban education, the basic skills notion (narrowly defined as reading, writing, and arithmetic, or more broadly defined as health and nutritional development skills, paramedical and layman–level legal aid training), can be greatly facilitated by providing productive, positive learning experiences. We believe that this is particularly true if affective interpersonal skills are interwoven simultaneously with teacher-administrator inservice and become operational notions when students learn basic skills.

It is difficult to believe that an urban school could maximize any learning program without making serious efforts to humanize learning experiences and interactions between teachers and students. In most successful schools, there has been a sustained high level or increase in the positive, affective domain-oriented dimensions of teacher-student interac-

---

[36] Keith Martin, "The Arts, the Schools, and the Community Wide Resource Center," *Phi Delta Kappan* 56 (January 1975): 334.

[37] Thomas J. Cleaver, "What are the Basics in Public Education?" Paper delivered at the Texas Education Agency Conference on Teacher Education, San Antonio, Texas, October 1976, p. 1.

tions. Although the data are incomplete in these areas, this notion will be further substantiated.

Given the nature of urban environmental pressures, those skills that are necessary to survive in the urban environment are the basics. To narrowly define or confine the basics of reading and writing without concern for health and nutrition in the elementary years, and political, paralegal and medical insights in the secondary years, is a suppressive style of maintenance and a status quo form of education, which is what the basics will be if the above is not included. Given the realities of urban environments, basic skills as they are taught today are unrealistic and unresponsive to the real and complex needs of urban students.

An example of urban curriculum efforts in the area of fundamental basic skills programs is the Parkway Program in Philadelphia, where a core faculty provided instruction in the basic skills and course structures which were in their areas of expertise.[38] The Parkway Program was organized into four different kinds of educational communities and used community volunteers with special skills who offered on-site experiences and internships in academic, commercial, and vocational areas.

Another approach has been Jesse Jackson's PUSH (People United to Save Humanity) Program for Excellence, which has embarked on unique programs in several urban areas. This program was founded on the idea that the greatest deficiencies in our schools are spiritual rather than material.[39] Children need the kind of concern and supervision which provides (1) motivation, (2) care, (3) discipline, and sometimes (4) chastisement —all components of a love triangle between the home, the church, and the school.[40] The program designated the development of a positive school atmosphere which is necessary in order to allow students to practice the "basics."

We keep saying that Johnny can't read because he's deprived, because he's hungry, because he's discriminated against. We say that Johnny can't read because his daddy is not in the home. Well, Johnny learns to play basketball without daddy. We do best what we do most, and for many of our children that is playing ball. One of the reasons Johnny does not read well is Johnny doesn't practice reading.[41]

In Milwaukee, Wisconsin, another unique alternative school, the "Commando Academy," has been developed to serve 10– to 17–year-olds

[38] Staples, p. 422.

[39] Eugene E. Eubanks and Daniel U. Levin, "The Push Program for Excellence in Big-City Schools," *Phi Delta Kappan* 58 (January 1977): 383.

[40] Ibid., p. 384.

[41] William Raspberry, "Racism Victims," *The Washington Post*, 8 March 1976.

who are parolees or ex-youth offenders.[42] The program was designed to provide basic skills of reading, writing, and mathematics to go along with "street" skills. The curriculum and learning experiences have been characterized by innovative instructional techniques, such as using dice to teach probability or pool shooting to teach geometry.

Another urban curriculum development effort was a program called the Newark Living Studies Center, in Newark, Delaware. The central aim on this project was to develop a curriculum based on high–interest activities outside the conventional school environment. The curriculum served as its own reinforcement; that is, instead of using high–interest activities to reinforce low interest, the program attempted to build living studies directly into the high interest activities themselves.

Communication Skills. It is clear that the urban environment contains a number of lifestyles, both in the context of ethnic-racial diversities and in terms of socioeconomic classifications or cleavages. This "hetero-mix" demands that people reach understandings with each other and to learn to build relationships. Urban students must have communication skills in order to accomplish these goals.

Traditionally, school curricula have used language arts, English, foreign language, and speech components to provide the necessary communication skills for students. However, one of the problems of communication skills training has been its failure to take into account the cultural, ethnic, or racial nature of the communicative task.

Curriculum experiences for students living in heterogeneous environments, particularly those in highly congested or heavily populated areas, must include building communication bridges to other people through the development of specific skills for multicultural or transracial contexts. Smith points out that communication skills in these contexts must take into account ethnic language styles and context, ethnic perspectives, symbols and racism, stereotypes, universal contexts for speaking, structure, form and content, symbolism, listening, and nonverbal communication styles.[43]

Within the various cultural contexts, languages, bilingualism, and multidialecticism are of major significance. Our emphasis here will primarily reflect the need for generic communication skills development and training as active components within a comprehensive urban curriculum, regardless of the language delivery mode.

    [42] Edward F. DeRouche and Jules J. Modlinski, "Commando Academy: From Clashes to Classrooms," *Educational Leadership* 34 (1977): 429.
    [43] Arthur L. Smith, *Transracial Communication* (Englewood Cliffs, N.J.: Prentice Hall, 1973), pp. 9-21.

Efforts to develop transcultural and transracial generic communicative skills as part of a curriculum program seem to be rare. Two interesting efforts related to language and communication skills have been the "World of Villages" learning experiences in the El Paso, Texas school district and "People Place" in the Houston, Texas, school district.[44] Both programs combine unique multicultural learning experiences from cultural contexts of different countries. These experiences develop skills in vocabulary, stereotype analysis, observation, listening, developmental perception, oral-aural activities, reading, and nonverbal communication skills; however, it is highly probable that most of the curriculum development in this area will have to be done from the ground up.

Problem-Solving and Decision-Making Social Action Skills. Most highly populated urban areas in America present their populations with daily tasks in solving problems, making decisions, and adopting a course of social action for resolution of problems. These tasks are similar to those faced by others living outside urban environments, in terms of methodology; however, they do demand the processing of radically different kinds of data and content as they relate to the nature of the urban environment and, obviously, to different kinds of problems.

Perhaps the nature of the urban atmosphere makes problem-solving, decision-making, and social action in big cities different. Nonetheless, the students who must face these tasks daily must be equipped to sustain themselves. In the past, schools attempted to teach additional information (knowledge) to individuals, but did not provide practical and utilitarian skills for dealing with problems and selecting a course of action.

The complexity of social action in urban environments demands that people learn to process divergent kinds of information through divergent interdisciplinary frameworks in order to make the individual a responsive social actor. Schools have not done well in providing students with these needed socialization processes or models, nor have parents had a commendable track record in this area. In the future, in order for various aspects of curricula to be functional for students, they will need to reflect learning experiences which engender and develop social action skills.

A few curriculum development efforts have provided some interesting models and processes that could be significant in the further generation of learning experiences of this type. Among such skills that reflect needs are social inquiry, value inquiry, and value clarification.[45] Another perspective

---

[44] Robert C. McKean and Bob L. Taylor, "Multicultural Learning," *Educational Leadership* 34 (1977): 479.

[45] James A. Banks and Ambrose H. Clegg, Jr., *Teaching Strategies for the Social Studies: Inquiry, Valuing, and Decision-Making* (Reading, Mass.: Addison-Wesley, 1977), pp. 481-518.

of decision-making skills is illustrated in the following process described by Woodley and Driscoll: identifying the occasion for a decision, recognizing values implicit in a decision situation, seeking and finding alternatives; creating alternatives, predicting consequences of alternatives, weighing alternatives and selecting one course of action, determining appropriate action to implement the decision, taking action to implement the decision, reflecting on the decision action and results.[46]

One interesting curriculum prototype for exploring the development of these skills was the Institute for Political and Legal Education (IPLE). This curriculum model was used in over twenty high schools in New Jersey and was a pilot project in several other states. The learning experiences themselves consisted of basic units in voter education, governmental decision-making, and individual rights. The results of the pilot curriculum project indicated not only increases in political and legal knowledge, but also greater activity in decision-making affairs as they related to the students, both in the schools and the communities at large.

Another project in Grand Rapids, Michigan, used the concept of the educational park where students attended classes in social studies and areas considered avant garde at the time, such as filmmaking, anthropology, value clarification, and social activism.[47] The result of this project was an increase in certain areas of utilitarian social skills.

The Cambridge Pilot School was an alternative experience working primarily with students in grades 9-12. This curriculum effort was characterized by informal relationships and emphasis on participation, decision-making, and respect for cultural diversity.[48] Among the specific curriculum offerings were courses and experiences in neighborhood studies, real people, crafts, Third World and United States history. Learning experiences also included seminars in skill areas such as listening and helping. The primary focus was to help urban students gain control over decisions affecting their lives and develop a conscience of community.

Other efforts in consumer education skills have also proved successful as models for future curriculum development efforts.

Occupation-Career Identity Awareness and Development Skills. In many instances, conditions within our urban environments reflect the immediate need for students and other urban residents to be prepared to act

[46] Celeste P. Woodley and Laura A. Driscoll, "A Model and Suggestions for Evaluating Decision-Making Skills," *Developing Decision-Making Skills,* ed. Dana G. Kurtman (Arlington, Va.: National Council for the Social Studies, 1977), p. 238.

[47] Kay Dodge, "Social Education in an Educational Park," *Social Education* 38 (March 1974): 252.

[48] Pilot School Staff Members, "Social Education in the Cambridge Pilot School," *Social Education* 38 (March 1974): 250.

as productive members of our society. Traditionally, our schooling response has been a dangerously nonproductive cleavage between academic subjects or intellectual learning experiences and vocational offerings of supposedly less academic or intellectual substance. Curriculum, particularly at the secondary level, is often divided into disciplines. Given the current social and economic conditions, a new approach to occupation and career awareness is needed in order to prepare students responsibly. Skill development is needed in the areas of career selections, interviewing processes, the researching of occupational literature and data, and test taking. Without these skills, the competitive nature of our society, along with its ethnic, racial, and social biases, often render students in urban areas helpless and unable to become productive members of society. We do not propose that this kind of curriculum be developed and delivered only at the secondary level; rather, we see these experiences existing throughout schools at all levels, from K-12. This is as much an affective challenge in curriculum development as it is cognitive.

Among the efforts to develop these learning experiences has been "Adopt a School," a recent joint venture between corporate executives and the Dallas, Texas, school district. Companies involved in the project allow employees time off to work as teacher aides in classrooms and to help prepare students for the world of work.[49]

Another project in Dallas that has been operating with significant impact has been the Skyline Career Development Center. This project provides a curriculum concept that meshes academic studies and a choice of twenty-four career clusters or fields.[50] Students are selected for the program through several evaluation channels, including self-discipline, emotional maturity, and past achievement. The goal of the program is to provide students with intellectual and occupation-oriented, marketable combinations of skills.

Unique among the various curriculum development efforts is project "Best" (Better Education Through Service and Training). The curriculum experiences in this project have been designed with a special family-like learning unit.[51] Project Best, a motivation and career preparation program for girls who were not doing well in regular school settings, emphasized basic skill development and career introduction.

Nationwide development of the "alternative school" and "magnet school" concepts, particularly in urban areas, has made it useful to develop

---

[49] "City Schools," *Newsweek,* 12 December 1977, p. 68.
[50] Nolan Estes, "Using the Rand D. Approach in Improving Urban Education," *Educational Leadership* 34 (1977): 266.
[51] Staples, p. 424.

thematic curricula and pool resources for concentrated learning efforts in such fields as allied health, engineering, the performing arts, science, and mathematics. We hope that this trend will lead to future efforts to create realistic learning environments for allowing students to become productive human beings.

The skill and knowledge development clusters that have been described briefly are representative and not exhaustive. Many possible clusters or combinations of clusters could be utilized as models for the development of urban curricula. The clusters themselves represent an orientation in terms of goals, objectives, and skills, toward significant new directions for learning in urban schools. The curriculum projects and programs that are described are only representative of programmatic curricula.

Incumbent in nearly all of the programmatic responses in urban curricula mentioned above were substantial efforts to integrate and incorporate the urban area and its resources in various kinds of cooperative partnerships. The task of involving the city in a cooperative and integrative fashion for expanding the learning experiences of urban students has been exciting and challenging and, at the same time, represented an epitome of resourcefulness. The key to meeting this challenge was in the skillfulness of urban educators and various members of the urban community in developing learning experiences that were reflective of urban students' needs.

The following ideas offer a suggested process for assisting urban educators in developing learning experiences drawing from the urban environment and its resources.

Step 1. Develop working relationships through an urban curriculum task force between instructional strategists, curriculum specialists, parents, students, administrators, and concerned community people in various curriculum areas for the introduction and implementation of the new curriculum dimensions into older and traditional curriculum areas such as language arts, reading, math, science, special education, business and career education, the arts, music, social studies, and physical education, or develop entirely new areas of curriculum.

Step 2. Based upon stated goal directives and outcomes, the curriculum task force should begin to explore and design experimental, urban-focused prototypical learning experiences and activities, and perform various analyses of the learning tasks that would be required to achieve the desired levels of skill attainment and knowledge development.

Step 3. Use the perspectives of task force members and the analysis of learning tasks, identify and design various configurating and alternative ways of reaching the desired goals, objectives, and skills and knowledge areas. This step involves the generation of learning ideas and matching them to resources in the community and vice versa. Factors to be considered during this step are distance-time relationships, time availability, scheduling, availability of personnel outside of the school district, personnel compensation, school-business trade–offs, work–study, internships, practicums, part-time employment, facilities, laboratories, cooperative management schemes, accreditation, certification, and transportation.

Step 4. Pilot prototype and field testing of the new curriculum with research, demonstration, and evaluation components installed.

Step 5. Develop a timetable for the introduction and inclusion of the new learning experiences with adequate support systems under very careful supervision. Three of the most crippling obstacles to a major curriculum development process inside an already established curriculum in an urban school or school district have been: (a) the lack of total commitment to important decision making, which in turn results in only partial or token project development; (b) the inability to clearly describe all of the different groups and individuals involved in the curriculum development process, as well as in the transitional state, and their roles after the prototype or demonstration phase has been completed; (c) the inability to promote or create positive working relationships between new content area specialists and teachers.

Step 6. Initiate the process of faculty and staff development for the new curriculum dimensions. This staff development should include all people who are connected in any way with the curriculum change, implementation process management and evaluation phases.[52]

Looking in retrospect at ideas or proposed processes that attempt to explain and coordinate human behaviors, it becomes clear that the most significant explanations and processes are ongoing and never-ending. The tasks involved in urban curriculum development must also be ongoing and never-ending.

---

[52] Anderson, p. 17.

4
Financing for Primary and Secondary Education in Urban Areas

Mark Gellerson and Claude Mayberry, Jr.

In recent years, the problem of how to finance public education has been widely debated. While this problem does not merely apply to urban schools, the issues it raises are particularly complex with respect to such schools, and an adequate solution is difficult to determine. Urban school financial problems can be analyzed most appropriately within the context of the financial difficulties which plague urban areas in general. The migration of relatively affluent city residents and businesses from the inner cities to the suburbs and from the "snowbelt" to the "sunbelt" regions has depleted the economic base upon which cities depend for tax revenues. This problem is exacerbated by the fact that the city residents who remain—many of whom simply cannot afford to leave—are precisely those who require the greatest amount of certain public services, such as welfare, medical care, and training. At the same time, the process of urban decay itself often leads to an increased need for other public services, such as police and fire protection. Thus, while the economic bases—and, hence, the resources to generate tax revenue—of many urban areas have stagnated or declined, public expenditures in urban areas have continued to increase. Urban schools are, therefore, faced with the difficult task of competing with other necessary local government services for a limited amount of local tax revenues.

Current Methods and Criticisms of Local School Finance

Methods

The principal source of funds for primary and secondary education is the local property tax.[1] State funding provides a lesser source of revenues and is usually in the form of grants to (1) support basic educational programs in all districts of the state, (2) fund special programs or services, or

(3) reduce differences in school districts' abilities to raise tax revenues. Since some state funding is supplied to all school districts (types (1) and (2) above) while equalization payments (type (3) above) are relatively small, only a limited degree of fiscal equalization is accomplished by state funding. Finally, federal funding accounts for a much smaller share of public school spending than either local or state funding, and it is directed toward specific types of educational assistance. In general, such federal funding does not have an equalizing effect. Overall, it is the tax revenues raised by local property taxes that primarily determine the revenues available for spending on public education.

Criticisms

Since property tax revenues are *ceteris paribus* related to the property wealth of a given community, the result of this current method of local school finance is to make a community's per-student expenditures a positive function of its property wealth.[2] Many state constitutions—but not the federal Constitution—view quality education as a "fundamental right," the access to which should not depend on a "suspect classification." That is, children have a right to a quality education, and providing that education should not depend on the wealth of the community in which a child lives. To the extent that the quality of education can be measured by the level of educational expenditures,[3] the current method of local school finance is

---

[1] For instance, in 1971-1972, 55 percent of the revenues used by such schools were raised by the local school districts, with 82 percent of the revenues accounted for by local property taxes. Revenues provided by state and federal governments accounted for 39 percent and 6 percent, respectively, of public elementary and secondary school spending. The outstanding exception is Hawaii, where the school system is administered by the state and predominantly financed with state tax revenues.

[2] However, in many cases in which communities have large amounts of non-residential property wealth, the correlation between the property wealth and income of community residents is low. This is a factor which complicates the task of determining a more equitable means of financing local education.

[3] In fact, one of the major weaknesses in the argument against using the property tax to finance local schools has been the inability of researchers to clearly establish this link between educational expenditures and the quality (or quantity) of educational outputs, where outputs are measured by test scores. Such major studies as those by James S. Coleman et al (*Equality of Educational Opportunity*, Washington: U.S. Office of Education, 1966) and Harvey Averch and others (*How Effective is Schooling? A Critical Review and Synthesis of Research Findings*, Santa Monica: RAND Corporation, 1922) have typically found that students' socioeconomic status and family characteristics "explain" most of their achievements in school. Expenditures on particular educational inputs appear to be relatively unimportant. In a recent work by Richard J. Murnane (*The Impact of School Resources on the Learning of Inner-City Children*, Cambridge: Ballinger, 1975), the author has established a link between

clearly at variance with this constitutional view of education as a fundamental right. This is the essential criticism of the existing method of school
finance and provides the basic rationale for several state supreme court
decisions declaring the existing method of local school finance to be
unconstitutional.[4]

Additional opposition to this current method of school finance stems
from the belief that the property tax *per se* is a "bad" tax. That is, the
property tax, as typically levied, is thought to be a regressive tax[5] that
imposes a relatively heavier burden on those with lower incomes. In addition, it has often been singled out as one of the causes of urban decay.[6]

Land is assumed to be fixed in supply so that the burden of the tax
that falls on land cannot be shifted and is, therefore, distributed progressively according to the distribution of income from wealth. The supply of
capital improvements (buildings) is, however, considered to be perfectly
elastic[7] over the relevant time period. This means that an increase in
property taxes results in the quantity of improvements being reduced to
the point that the price of improvements is increased by the amount of the
tax increase. Thus, the net-of-tax price of (or return to) improvements remains constant, while consumers of housing pay the full amount of the tax
increase. That is, the tax is fully shifted forward. Since families with lower
incomes are thought to spend, on the average, a higher fraction of their
current incomes on housing than do families with higher incomes, the

---

the learning of reading and mathematical skills on the one hand, and teacher quality
on the other (as evaluated by principals). But since teacher quality is not related to
years of training and only partially related to experience, it is not possible, even in
this case, to conclude that greater expenditures result in better education.

[4] Some of the major decisions have been *Serrano v. Priest* (California, 1971),
Van Dusartz v. Hatfield (Minnesota, 1971), *Rodriguez v. San Antonio Independent
School District* (Texas, 1971), and *Robinson v. Cahill* (New Jersey, 1972). For a
general discussion of some of the implications of these decisions, see Joel Berke and
John Callahan, "*Serrano v. Priest:* Milestone or Millstone for School Finance,"
Journal of Public Law, 1972; and Ferdinand P. Schoettle, "Judicial Requirements for
School Finance and Property Tax Redesign: The Rapidly Evolving Case Law,"
National Tax Journal (September 1972).

[5] See, for example, A. M. Agapos and Paul R. Dunlap, "Elimination of Urban
Blight Through Inverse Proportional Ad Valorem Property Taxation," *American
Journal of Economics and Sociology* (April 1973), pp. 142-152.

[6] Examples of the traditional view of property tax incidence are found in Richard
Musgrave et al., "Distribution of Tax Payments by Income Groups, A Case Study
for 1948," *National Tax Journal* (March 1951), pp. 1-53; and Dick Netzer, *Economics
of the Property Tax* (Washington, D.C.: Brookings Institution, 1966).

[7] However, empirical results provided in Larry Orr, "The Incidence of Differential
Property Taxes on Urban Housing," *National Tax Journal* (September, 1968), pp.
253-262; and in Frank de Leeuw and Nkanta F. Ekanem, "The Supply of Rental
Housing," *American Economic Review* (December 1971), pp. 806-817; indicate that
the supply of housing is less than perfectly elastic, at least in the short run.

burden of the property tax on structures is assumed to be distributed regressively.

With respect to taxes on nonresidential property, it is assumed that the tax on land is not shifted and is borne according to the distribution of property wealth. The tax on improvements is assumed to be shifted forward in the form of higher prices of outputs. In this case, the burden of the tax on improvements is distributed progressively or regressively according to whether consumption of the good in question increases or decreases relative to increases in income. In reality, the degree of competition in the market of the good in question affects the ability of the taxed firm to shift this part of the tax forward. That is, forward shifting is more likely for goods produced and sold in local markets and is correspondingly less likely for goods exported to other markets (unless most of the producers of the goods competing in such export markets are subject to the same rate of property tax).

This traditional view of property tax incidence is by no means universally accepted. In fact, during the last few years a substantial literature challenging this view has developed.[8] This revisionist approach generally concludes that the burden of the property tax is not as regressively distributed as previously thought. This view holds that the *average* burden of the property tax (across the country) is borne by all owners of capital; not just those owning land or improvements, but those owning other nontaxed forms of capital as well. Specifically, the average return earned by capital is reduced by the average tax rate; the burden of the average tax is distributed according to the distribution of income from wealth. Differentials in the tax rate on residential housing across communities or regions can lead to some forward shifting to the consumers of housing. But proponents of the new view cite evidence[9] that the income elasticity of housing expenditures, when measured by using permanent rather than current income, is greater than once believed. Thus, even this burden is not unduly regressive. Regarding tax differentials that affect commercial and industrial property, the new view emphasizes the need for firms to exercise market

[8] See, for example, Peter Mieszkowski, "The Property Tax: An Excise or Profits Tax?" *Journal of Public Economics* (April 1972), pp. 73-96; Henry J. Aaron, *Who Pays the Property Tax?* (Washington, D.C.: Brookings Institution, 1975); and Helen Ladd, "The Role of the Property Tax: A Reassessment," *Broad Based Taxes*, ed. Richard Musgrave (Baltimore: Johns Hopkins University Press, 1973), pp. 39-86.
[9] See Richard Muth, "The Demand for Non-Farm Housing," *The Demand for Durable Goods*, ed. Arnold Harberger (Chicago: University of Chicago Press, 1960), pp. 29-96; and Frank de Leeuw, "The Demand for Housing: A Review of Cross-Sectional Evidence," *Review of Economics and Statistics* 11 (February 1971): 1-10.

power or to act collusively if they are to accomplish much forward shifting. In other words, competitive market forces are thought to significantly restrict shifting.[10]

The property tax has often been criticized because of its undesirable effects on urban development. Specifically, some studies[11] indicate that in urban areas the assessment ratio, that is, the ratio of assessed value to market value, is lower on land (especially vacant lots) than on improvements. Such relative underassessment of land in urban areas may reduce the incentive for intensive land use and encourage speculators to keep land idle. Conversely, high taxes in improvements may discourage the upgrading of properties in urban areas.[12] Evidence also indicates that tax rates are often higher in low-income or downward-transitional neighborhoods than they are in high-income neighborhoods.[13] This is probably due to the failure of local governments to reassess property values in accordance with neigh-

---

[10] Most studies of property tax incidence fail to consider: (1) the imputed rent earned by owner-occupiers; (2) low-income families living in mobile homes which typically are undertaxed; and (3) property taxes paid on second homes by families that, on the average, have high incomes. These factors provide additional reasons why the burden of the property tax may be less regressively distributed than previously thought, and they are valid regardless of whether the traditional new view of property tax incidence is held. Also, the increased use of "circuit breakers" may reduce the regressivity of the property tax. Such circuit breakers provide home owners with relief if their property taxes exceed a certain percentage of their income. This relief is usually not in the form of direct payments from the state or of credits against state taxes. Typically, there are restrictions on the age and income of people who can use circuit breakers. In a few states, renters are also eligible for circuit-breaker relief. In this case, property taxes are estimated as a certain fraction of the rent paid (thereby forward shifting of the tax is assumed). While the goals of such relief are praiseworthy, it is not clear why such relief should be in the form of complete tax forgiveness rather than simple tax deferral until death. As it is, such circuit breakers tend to provide excessive benefits to those with fluctuating incomes and to those who choose to make large expenditures on housing. For a discussion of circuit-breaker programs in various states, see the Advisory Commission on Intergovernmental Relations, "Financing Schools and Property Tax Relief" (Washington, D.C.: ACIR, January, 1973).

[11] Frederick D. Stocker, "Property Taxation, Land Use, and Rationality in Urban Growth Policy," *Property Taxation, Land Use, and Public Policy,* ed. Arthur Lynn (Madison: University of Wisconsin Press, 1973), pp. 112-136.

[12] Findings indicate that the fear of reassessment may result in a stronger disincentive against property improvements than do actual reassessment practices themselves. Specifically, a survey of assessment practices in ten large United States cities indicated that improvements costing less than $10,000 led to upward reassessments within three years in only 10 percent of the cases. See George Peterson et al., *Property Taxes, Housing, and the Cities* (Lexington, Massachusetts: D. C. Heath Company, 1973). Results of this study indicate that it is the generally high property taxes found in blighted areas, rather than the threat of reassessment, which produce the major disincentive against improvements.

[13] This is a practical reason why the property tax may be regressive, despite new theoretical arguments to the contrary.

borhood changes. The result is clearly to accelerate urban decay where it has already begun.

Finally, the property taxes may contribute to urban decay simply because tax rates are higher in central cities than in surrounding suburbs or rural areas. Although cities typically have above-average per capita property tax bases (relative to the state in which they are located), they also have much above-average tax rates because of greater public expenditure requirements. The per unit costs of providing public services tend to be greater in urban areas, and more services are usually required. With respect to education, for example, not only are routine capital and operating costs more expensive in urban areas, but there also tend to be higher percentages of students, such as retarded and disturbed children, who need high-cost, special education programs.[14] The fact that more public services (not just education) must be provided at higher costs in urban areas has led to the recognition that cities face a "municipal overburden." To the extent that this overburden results in higher property tax rates, there is an increased incentive for business establishments and residents (who can afford to be mobile) to locate outside urban areas.

In summary, the current method of financing public education is criticized mainly because a district's ability to raise revenues for education is dependent upon its property wealth. Moreover, the property tax is thought by some to have undesirable equity effects, and the manner by which it is currently administered may contribute to the process of urban decay. With this overview of current methods and criticisms of local school finance as a background, alternative methods of financing local schools will be outlined and evaluated. Emphasis is placed on how well such alternatives meet the needs of urban schools.

Alternative Methods of Financing Local Schools

Before any alternative methods of financing local schools are considered, the reader must realize one important point. These alternatives have been suggested as a means of reducing the disparities in funding

---

[14] For example, in Betsy Levin et al., *The High Cost of Education in Cities* (Washington, D.C.: Urban Institute, 1973), the authors found that per pupil operating expenditures were $13 greater, $58 greater, and $277 greater in cities than in slow-growing suburbs, fast-growing suburbs, and rural areas, respectively. These higher costs primarily reflect higher instructional costs. Capital costs were also higher in city schools because of higher site acquisition and construction costs. For a discussion of both the higher costs associated with special education programs and disproportionate numbers of special education students found in urban areas, *see* Robert D. Reischauer and Robert W. Hartman, *Reforming School Finance* (Washington, D.C.: Brookings Institution, 1973), pp. 63-65.

which result from the great variations in assessed values per pupil across school districts. To the extent that such alternatives involve a redistribution of revenues from high property wealth districts to low ones, the urban districts are likely to suffer since they typically have above-average per-pupil property wealth. Conversely, most alternatives are not designed to deal with the problems resulting from the higher costs of education in urban areas. It is this fact which makes the development of an acceptable method of financing for local schools in general, and urban schools in particular, so difficult.

Court decisions ruling against the constitutionality of existing methods of financing local education have not suggested suitable alternative methods. This responsibility has been left to the various state and local governments. These decisions have, however, established the general direction of school finance reform. While not requiring equal educational expenditures across districts, these decisions have established that alternative methods of finance should ensure that the provision of quality education does not depend on the community's property wealth.[15] As a result, several alternative methods of school finance, or methods of modifying the current system of finance, have been suggested. The major alternatives are (1) state assumption, (2) district power equalizing, (3) redistricting, (4) vouchers, and (5) amending state equalization formulas.

State Assumption

The rationale behind state assumption of the role of financing local education is clear. By collecting taxes on a state-wide basis and redistributing them according to educational needs, the disparities resulting from wide variations in local property-tax wealth are reduced. Typically, advocates of this approach suggest using increased state income taxes to replace funding currently derived from local property taxes.[16] Not only would funding disparities be reduced,[17] but, according to the conventional

---

[15] Educational expenditures can depend on the level of wealth in the state as a whole, however.

[16] For example, the Fleishman Commission, which studied the question of how to reform local school finance in New York State, recommended full state funding, with all districts being brought up to the 65th percentile of spending. The Commission further recommended initially replacing local property taxes with a state property tax, which itself would be gradually replaced by increased state income taxes.

[17] It is not at all clear that equal levels of taxes and expenditures across districts are completely desirable. In fact, there is an efficiency-related argument to the contrary. Variations in taxes and the levels of provision of public services allow families, to some extent, to choose which combination they prefer. In effect, such variations allow a competitive, private market determination of the optimal bundle of local

view of tax incidence, the overall burden of taxes would be distributed more equitably since progressive income taxation replaces regressive property taxation. Presumably, local control would be maintained over decisions relating to curriculum, hiring and firing, and choices relating to the day-to-day operation of schools.

State assumption would reduce the importance of local property wealth as a determinant of local educational expenditures. However, there are several difficulties with such a plan. First, in order for state assumption to be politically feasible, total spending on local education would almost certainly have to increase considerably. Reducing levels of spending significantly below current levels in high expenditure districts would be strenuously resisted by the people living in such districts. It is these people who are apt to exercise the most political power. As a result, state assumption would likely cause an upward equalizing of school district expenditures. The result would be higher educational expenditures and higher state taxes.[18] Second, whether or not state assumption would benefit or harm urban schools is not clear. Some studies indicate that as a result of state assumption, taxes paid in urban areas to finance schooling will increase by more than the revenues made available by the state for financing education.[19] Thus, the financial problems facing urban schools may be increased by state assumption.[20] Finally, the reduction of local property taxes would result in substantial capital gains for property owners and possibly encourage them to hold urban land idle for speculative purposes.

public goods to be provided. People can "vote with their feet," by moving to the locality which provides that bundle of public goods and taxes which best meets their needs and financial abilities. This is essentially the hypothesis put forth by Charles Tiebout in "A Pure Theory of Local Expenditures," *Journal of Political Economy* (October 1956), pp. 416-424. Clearly, some people cannot afford to be mobile and, thus, this mechanism does not work efficiently in all cases. But it does provide some justification for variations in local expenditures.

[18] Hartman and Reischauer, *op. cit.*, pp. 81-82, estimate that equalizing up to the 90th percentile would have resulted in increased educational spending of $7 billion in the United States in 1970. As a result, total state taxes would have had to increase by 14.5 percent.

[19] See the Advisory Commission on Intergovernmental Relations, *loc. cit.*, and Callahan and Berke, *loc. cit.* In the latter study, the authors conclude that in only two of thirteen cities analyzed will increases in revenues exceed increases in taxes.

[20] Court decisions have not forbidden the distribution of financial resources on the basis of cost or need. Thus, plans for state assumption could allow for the higher costs of urban education. For example, students with special educational needs could be given a higher weight when determining average daily attendance figures.

District Power Equalizing

Under district power equalizing, the state, in effect, ensures that every school district has the same ability (or power) to raise property tax revenues.[21] That is, the state ensures each district a certain per-pupil property tax revenue, and the size of this revenue varies positively with the property tax rate at which the district is willing to tax itself. If the tax revenues raised by applying the tax rate to the local property-tax base are less than the amount the state guarantees, the state will provide payments to make up the difference. Conversely, if locally raised revenues exceed the amount guaranteed by the state, these "extra" revenues will be transferred to the state government and ultimately redistributed to districts to which the state makes payments.

The strength of this plan is that it maintains local choice while removing the constraint which local property wealth places on this choice. There are, however, a number of problems associated with power equalizing. First, it will make state financial planning more difficult since the required level of state government expenditures will not be known until localities decide on their tax rates. Second, total expenditures on local education will likely rise since it will be politically more expedient for the state to guarantee districts a revenue-raising ability which is greater than that currently enjoyed by districts with average wealth.[22] Third, it will be difficult to determine an appropriate measure of a district's fiscal capacity. Assessed property values per pupil are the most often suggested measure. This may be inappropriate for a number of reasons. The composition of the property tax base may need to be accounted for. That is, those districts in which a relatively large fraction of property wealth consists of commercial and industrial property may be able to "export" a larger share of property taxes than those districts with predominately residential properties. Those districts with a great ability to export taxes might be willing to tax themselves at high rates since they bear the burden of only a small

[21] See John E. Coons and others, *Private Wealth and Public Education* (Cambridge, Massachusetts: Harvard University Press, 1970).

[22] For example, in Robert Gilmer, "Predicting the Cost of Fiscal Equalization in School Finance," *Public Finance Quarterly* (July 1975), pp. 261-274, the author estimates that the adoption of district power equalizing—with a guaranteed tax base near the average tax base, with "extra" revenues returned to the state—would result in 4 percent higher educational costs in taxes. If a higher tax base is guaranteed, or if extra revenues are retained by localities, then the increase in educational costs would be even greater.

fraction of the taxes.[23] For the sake of equity, this export ability should be controlled—presumably with those districts having greater ability to export taxes being guaranteed lower tax revenues at any given tax rate. Moreover, the correlation between the property wealth of a district and the income of the residents may be weak.[24] This is because valuable commercial and industrial properties may be located in low-income districts. In such cases, district power equalizing will do little to improve the equity of local school finance. Finally, to the extent that variations in tax rates are capitalized in property values, the redistributive effect of district power equalizing will unduly burden and benefit high and low property-wealth districts, respectively.[25] Fourth, power equalizing might provide little help for urban schools because of their typically above-average per pupil property-tax wealth. Recognition of the higher costs of urban education would be necessary. Fifth, the price of public education in wealthy districts will be greatly increased; as a reaction, such districts might decide to tax themselves at low rates. The ultimate effect could be greatly increased attendance in private schools.

Redistricting

Another way to reduce disparities in the abilities of school districts to raise local tax revenues for education is to create larger districts which

[23] A study by John Bowman, "Tax Exportability, Intergovernmental Aid and School Finance Reform," *National Tax Journal* (June 1974), pp. 163-173, presents results that indicate that school districts with relatively high abilities to export property taxes do tax themselves at higher rates.

[24] See Michael J. Churgin and others, "A Statistical Analysis of School Finance Decisions: On Winning Battles and Losing Wars," *Yale Law Journal* (June 1972), pp. 1303-1341. In a sample of 130 towns and cities in Connecticut, the authors found that there was no significant correlation between the percent of families below the poverty line and property wealth per pupil. The authors did, however, find a significant *positive* correlation between the percent of families below the poverty line and business property wealth.

[25] If property taxes are capitalized, then the property values in districts with high property wealth and low tax rates will be reduced as a result of the adoption of district power equalizing. Conversely, property values will increase in previously high tax districts. Thus, residents in high property-wealth districts eventually pay higher tax rates and incur capital losses. For findings which support the idea that rate differentials are capitalized, see Albert Church, "Capitalization of the Effective Property Tax Rate on Single Family Residences," *National Tax Journal* (March 1974). One of the greatest difficulties in doing such studies is to adequately sort out the capitalization of tax differentials from the capitalization of variations in local public good provision. See, for example, Wallace E. Oates, "The Effect of Property Taxes and Local Public Spending on Property Values: An Empirical Study of Tax Capitalization and the Tiebout Hypothesis," *Journal of Political Economy* (November/December 1969), pp. 957-971.

are more homogeneous in property wealth. In theory, this might appear to be a simple and satisfactory approach; in practice, however, this approach would be exceedingly difficult to implement. It might be unpopular simply because residents fear the loss of local control of education. Also, residents living in high-wealth districts would resist attempts to merge their districts with low-wealth ones. Clearly, in many cases merging would be impractical and possibly exacerbate racial or ethnic prejudices. District boundaries might have to be changed periodically in order to account for changing distributions of property wealth—an exceedingly difficult task. Finally, such redistricting would do little or nothing to ease the financial problems faced by urban areas.

Vouchers

Voucher plans represent the most radical type of local school finance reform since they would alter not only the method of financing local education but also the system by which such education is provided. Such plans would make the family, rather than the local school district or the state, the educational decision-maker. Specifically, states would provide payments, or vouchers, to the families of primary and secondary students. These vouchers would be used to purchase education,[26] thus removing the influence of local property wealth on educational expenditures.[27] In addition, vouchers might increase the quality of schooling, since they will encourage competition among schools and therefore provide students and families with a greater variety of choice concerning the type of education to be received.[28]

Voucher plans have been criticized by some because they might encourage (or permit) various forms of segregation. However, limited evidence gathered from an experimental voucher program in Alum Rock, California,

[26] For an early discussion of vouchers, see Milton Friedman, *Capitalism and Freedom* (Chicago: University of Chicago Press, 1962). For a more complete analysis, see Center for the Study of Public Policy, "Educational Vouchers: A Preliminary Report on Financing Education by Payments to Parents" (Cambridge, Massachusetts: The Center, 1970). A type of voucher plan for local education was considered in Michigan in 1978; but the voters rejected it in November, 1978.

[27] However, family wealth might become an important determinant of educational expenditures if families with higher incomes tend to supplement vouchers. Some voucher plans attempt to prevent this by requiring schools which participate in voucher programs to accept only voucher payments.

[28] The state legislature of Indiana is considering a proposal which will require that state funds be used via a voucher system to non-public schools meeting certain criteria. Parents would be permitted to enroll their children in public schools of their choice within their district, or could require the school district to approve the transfers of their children and funds to schools outside their districts.

indicates that this has not been the case.[29] For instance, results indicate that only 15 percent of the participating students were enrolled in schools other than those to which they would have normally been assigned. Clearly, however, the limited scope of such experimental programs reduces the significance of any finding. With respect to the problems facing urban schools, voucher programs might be particularly suitable since it would be relatively easy to vary the amount of the voucher payment in order to account for higher costs or increased expenditure needs.

Amending Equalization Formulas

As presently administered, state aid programs for education have little equalizing effect. Flat grants, which provide payments to all school districts according to the number of students or personnel employed, are not equalizing.[30] Foundation grants in theory are equalizing,[31] but in practice they are relatively ineffective since they are set at such low levels. By increasing the size of such state aid programs, states could ensure that all students receive an education of at least minimum quality (measured in terms of expenditures). If the minimum foundation level were raised significantly, educational disparities resulting from extreme interdistrict variations in per-pupil property wealth could be reduced considerably. Finally, such state aid programs could be easily adapted to meet the special problems of urban education which result from their greater expenditure requirement.

Evaluation and Recommendations

Evaluation

The previous two sections have outlined the problems associated with the current method of financing primary and secondary education and evaluated some of the proposed methods of reform. Special emphasis has been placed on considering the ways in which such reforms will or will not meet the special financial needs of urban schools. The present section will

---

[29] For more details, see Stephen Sugarman, "Family Choice: The Next Step in the Quest for Equal Educational Opportunity?" *Law and Contemporary Problems* (Winter/Spring 1974), pp. 513-565.

[30] Slight equalization might result if, as is the case in some states, the size of per-student grants were to vary according to educational costs in the district or the type of pupil being educated.

[31] Foundation plans guarantee each district a minimum amount of revenues per pupil to be spent on education. The actual per-pupil foundation grant equals the difference between this guaranteed minimum and the actual revenue which the district can raise at a specified property tax rate.

first outline desirable characteristics for methods of local school finance and then suggest a method of financing which is particularly suited for the problems facing urban areas in general and urban schools in particular.

The principal factor which distinguishes the problem of financing urban schools from the problem of financing local education in general is clearly the urban areas' municipal overburden. Such an overburden exists because more public services are required in urban areas and because providing those services is usually more expensive there.

A fundamental principle of economics is that the market, through the price system, allocates resources efficiently. If people choose to live in urban areas and demand large quantities of expensive public services, they should be required to pay the full social cost of those services. Consequently, the costs to urban areas of municipal overburdens should not generally be subsidized by a higher level of government.[32] There are several reasons, however, why it is appropriate for higher levels of government to pay at least part of the costs of such overburdens. First, urban residents may not make explicit choices which lead to higher costs of public services provision. Many city residents cannot afford to be mobile and are unduly burdened by the high costs of public services just because they live in cities. Nor are city residents directly responsible for the fact that many of their children have learning problems which require expensive special education. Second, nonurban residents also benefit to some degree from the services provided in urban areas. They use transport systems, police protection, and cultural facilities. Thus, it is appropriate for nonurban residents to pay part of the costs of providing such services.[33] These are at least some of the factors which provide the economic justification for state or national aid to ease such overburdens.[34]

The second issue to be considered is how to design a system of school finance that ensures reasonable degrees of efficiency and fairness in the provision of education. This is not an easy task since, depending on one's definition of fairness, these two objectives can conflict. Typically, local choice is thought to be an effective means of ensuring the provision of an efficient level of local public services. This is because preferences are likely to be more homogeneous over a small locality and can be more accurately

[32] The problem of municipal overburden is complicated by the fact that services provided by the public sector in some cities are provided privately in other cities.

[33] This discussion relates to the city-suburb exploitation controversy. An analysis of this issue can be found in William B. Neenan, "Suburban-Central City Exploitation Thesis: One City's Tale," *National Tax Journal* (June 1970), pp. 117-139.

[34] This chapter considers only the need for aid to reduce educational overburdens. It may make more sense, however, to consider more comprehensive programs which relieve the general financial overburden under which cities labor.

determined by a local government. However, local choice may not lead to a "fair" interdistrict allocation of educational resources. In this respect, the basic question is whether inequality in school funding which results from local choice under a power equalizing plan is more or less fair than the imposed equality which might result from state assumption or voucher plans. In the case of education, fairness is not necessarily achieved by giving people equal means and then letting them do what they want. Power equalizing plans will not necessarily lead to a fair provision of education. This is because those people actually benefiting from the service, that is, children, have no way in determining its level of provision. If the role of education is to provide children with knowledge, skills, and abilities—to which all children have a fundamental right—then why should this right be abridged because adults in a local community do not have the desire or capacity to fully provide the necessary educational services? Conversely, why should some children be given a comparative educational advantage simply because adults so desire and have the capacity to accomplish it? [35] This suggests that public education is most appropriately thought of as a merit good, for which a higher level of government—less sensitive to parental and other taxpayers' pressures—can best determine the overall level of provision which is most appropriate for children. In summary, state control over general educational spending levels, and local control over the allocation of such spending, might come as close as possible to being a fair and efficient means of financing local education.

None of the alternative methods of school finance discussed above will directly mitigate the financial problems facing urban schools. [36] Urban schools are not so much burdened by the problem of low per-pupil property wealth, which is the essential problem for which alternative methods of finance are designed. Rather, the major problem facing urban schools is that of providing high-cost educational services when expenditure needs are growing more rapidly than local revenues. To ease this crunch, some

[35] A fairer allocation of resources to local education might result if a Rawlsian paradigm were applied. That is, funding decisions concerning local education would be made by adults in the absence of knowledge concerning whether these funds would be applied to their own children. For a more complete discussion of fairness in educational finance, see Stephan Michelson, "What is a 'Just' System for Financing Schools? An Evaluation of Alternative Reforms," *Law and Contemporary Problems* (Winter/Spring 1974), pp. 436-458.

[36] To the extent that state assumption of the role of financing local education results in a leveling of property tax rates, urban areas might indirectly benefit since urban residents and businesses could not avoid high taxes by moving to suburban or rural areas. However, as discussed above, some findings indicate that taxes will increase more than revenues in urban areas under state assumption.

type of special aid must be given to urban schools.[37] If states assume the role of determining general level expenditures, it should be relatively easy for allowances to be made for higher educational costs (through a cost index) and greater numbers of special education students (by weighing such students more heavily in attendance figures).

Recommendations

Given the above evaluation, what is the specific method of local school finance which will best meet both the general needs for reform and the specific problems facing urban schools? As discussed above, a fair yet efficient method of finance would be one that (1) reduces the ability of parents to give give their children a comparative educational advantage, (2) maintains local choice over curriculum and the allocation of revenues between alternative uses, and (3) allows for differences in educational costs and tasks. In other words, the state must assume the role of distributing funds for local education.

How should the state collect the additional revenues needed to support its financing role? Local property taxes could be replaced by state-wide site value (or land) tax,[38] and assessment practices could be revised so that the assessed value of land more accurately reflects the actual market value. The advantages of such a tax are many.[39] First, it would provide a stable source of tax revenues—more so, for instance, than a state income tax. Second, it would be a progressive tax—regardless of whether one supports the traditional view or the new view of property tax incidence. Third, it can easily be justified since the value of land is largely determined by conditions in the community as a whole. Fourth, and perhaps most important for our purposes, it would not discourage property improvements. It would encourage more intensive land use and reduce the practice of holding land idle for speculative purposes.[40] This method of taxation might help to

[37] In fact, such aid should not be restricted to urban schools, but rather should be provided to all districts faced with higher input costs and large numbers of special education students.

[38] A less extreme approach might be the adoption of a state-wide property tax which taxes land more heavily than improvements.

[39] For a discussion of site value taxes and an analysis of the redistribution of tax liabilities that would result from the switch to a site value tax, see Dean O. Popp and Frederick D. Sembold, "Redistribution of Tax Liabilities Under Site Value Taxation: A Survey of San Diego County," *American Journal of Economics and Sociology* (October 1972), pp. 427-437.

[40] One assumes, of course, that assessment practices will be improved so that land (especially idle land) is no longer relatively underassessed.

reverse the process of urban decay, or at least, it would not contribute to this process—as does the system of local property taxation as currently administered.

This method of financing local education must be coupled with special aid to urban schools. Such aid will serve to reduce somewhat the heavy financial burden which urban areas face as a result of the excessive costs of urban education. This aid may be in the form of a specific program directed only to education, or it may constitute part of a general program aimed at easing the financial plight of urban areas.

There are several other alternatives which, combined with the above recommendations, are worthy of consideration: (1) giving tax credits to industries and businesses that give money directly to the school district, (2) subjecting to local property taxes state and governmental agencies that own property within the urban district, (3) requiring those who work within the urban district and whose salaries are paid with tax money to live within the urban district, and (4) levying a tax for those who work within the city but who live outside the city limtis.

Finally, one should expect a leveling up of educational expenditures if this method of finance is to be politically feasible. As a result, the total costs of local education will increase. This is probably unavoidable and, indeed, is perhaps even desirable given the mandates handed down by several courts.[41]

Whereas all of the above suggestions warrant closer scrutiny, it is obvious that they all have positive and negative implications. The Institute for Urban Education and Human Resource Development described in Chapter Five proposes an excellent structure to further scrutinize these alternatives and the other proposals presented in this chapter.

[41] For a full disclosure of the court cases, the reader should review the cases listed in footnote 4.

5

Politics and the Curriculum

Claude Mayberry, Jr.

It is the system, not bricks and mortar, that will assure our children of a decent education.

Although it is a fundamental human right to learn, grow, and develop, it is not a legal guarantee. The judicial system has effected numerous changes relating to the equal opportunity to learn, but little has been done to encourage legislation guaranteeing equal access to that opportunity.

This chapter will review some of the legal actions, related to the themes of the previous chapters, which have greatly influenced education over the past quarter-century. It is an attempt to demonstrate that political influence has gone a long way to guarantee human rights and an individual's right to an education, but has done little to guarantee that the individual receive an education.[1] This chapter will further review the local level political process by observing how different groups use this process to maximize their positions in their respective school systems.

Review of Some Court Actions and Their Impact on Education

Rights of Parents

Education was once considered to be a privilege of the rich and an advantage to the poor. In the nineteenth century, the amount and type of education a child received was a very personal issue between the child, his parents, and the school. It was customary for a father to decide that he did not want his children to be educated by schools at all. For girls this was the rule rather than the exception. Once inside the school, however, the student

---

[1] An illustration of this is the number of urban students who have exercised their right to attend school, but who are allowed to graduate from high school with a fifth- or sixth-grade education. Obviously, this has national implications. But it is also obvious that state and federal legislation and the courts have placed most of their influence at the entrance and very little at the exit.

was considered to be under the total control of the teacher, whose word was law. By the same token, the local school district could dictate exactly what was to be taught. Thus, the term *in loco parentis* accurately described the relationship of the teacher to the child.

There have been many changes since those days. No longer does the teacher have the right to teach and discipline the student arbitrarily, and no longer does the parent have the right to dictate what the child will be taught. If parents have enough money, they may decide where their children are to be educated, but not whether they are to be educated. In the past ten years a number of court decisions have radically altered the relative standing of students, parents, and teachers within the educational system. Recent changes in school law, prompted in part by a number of law suits, have affected such areas as prayer, the salute to the flag, dress codes, married students, punishment, health, religion, suspension and expulsion practices, integration and desegration, student civil rights, and a host of other issues.

The image of the school district as being controlled by local parents and concerned citizens has been erroneous for years. Local districts are controlled by local people to a very limited degree. State and federal requirements have subverted much of the vaunted local control. Local control has been limited to minor issues which have been decided in accordance with existing law.[2] School boards who once dictated subject matter are now limited to textbook choices. Even the power to hire and fire teachers has been circumscribed. Ironically, in those areas where the local board has the authority to exercise power, the decisions have often been appealed to the courts, and these appeals have resulted in further erosion of the school board's authority.[3]

Schools still have the power to act *in loco parentis,* particularly in regard to discipline (for example, spanking) and health, for which the school has the right to act in the role of the parent regarding certain procedures.[4] Parents may be superseded in such instances in which proper health procedures are not being maintained within the home. This posture has come about since several court cases have upheld the rights of the school to require certain actions on the part of the parent in these areas and, when the parent has not performed appropriate actions, to take over these functions.[5]

[2] R. L. Mandel, "Student Rights, Legal Principles and Educational Policy," *Intellect* 103 (January 1975): 237.

[3] M. C. Nolte, "School Boards: Your Authority Has Just Been Restricted; School Board Members: Your Security Has Just Been Threatened," *American School Board Journal* 162 (April 1975): 33-35.

[4] R. S. Strahan, *Courts and Schools* (Lincoln, Neb.: Professional Educators' Publishing Co., 1973), pp. 21-22.

[5] Mandel, p. 237.

Parents are yet held responsible for the attendance of their children in the public school system. In most states the encouragement of truancy on the part of a minor is a misdemeanor; in some states it is a felony. In a number of recent cases, some dealing with school boycotts organized by parents, the courts have upheld that attendance is a responsibility of the parent.[6]

The school is responsible for any action by a student during the school day and stands in the place of the parent during school hours. On the other hand, the question of authority of the school and of the parent in case of off-school ground and after-school activities is not yet codified. The issue is difficult. At the present time, most court cases hold the school responsible for after-school activities, such as ball games, dances, and other extracurricular activities that are sponsored by the school, but not for activities occurring outside the school grounds.[7] A notable exception is the case of student actions on a school bus. Since a school bus serves as an extension of the school, if two students scuffle on a school bus, whether enroute to a school activity or to their homes, their actions are under the jurisdiction of the school. However, if the same two students scuffle as they walk home from school, they are not under the jurisdiction of the school, but rather that of their parents. The school cannot be held responsible for the actions of a child off the school grounds during his lunch hour, even if it is the practice of the school to allow students to leave the school grounds at lunch time. However, if the child is injured on the playground during the lunch hour, the school is responsible.[8]

During recent years, the authority of the school over its pupils in the field of civil liberties has been diminishing. Schools no longer can dictate the length and style of a student's hair or attire beyond general guidelines. Reasons cited for this change reflect the fact that school authorities had become so strong that the courts began to perceive the school as usurping the parental role. Courts heard several cases in which the parent and child both had found the child's dress and appearance to be acceptable but the school had not. In each case the court ruled that as long as the dress and hair length did not interfere with the learning process, they were the

[6] Strahan, pp. 21-22.

[7] The urban schools have lost revenues over the past ten years because they have had to cut back their sport activities. Normally, basketball and football games are played at night to induce larger attendances. However, many urban schools must play their games before it gets dark to maximize the safety of their students.

[8] E. M. Clayton and G. S. Jacobsen, "Analysis of Court Cases Concerned with Students' Rights," *NASSP Bulletin* 58 (February 1974): 52-53.

province of the student and his or her parents. It took several such cases to remove such codification from the school's domain.[9]

It has been a long-cherished tradition that schools be controlled by the communities which they serve. The states themselves exercised only minimal control of local districts until the twentieth century. The federal government only intervened to reassert local control. Since the turn of the century, education has become the prerogative of the state.

Before 1900 the only major court decision affecting local public education was the 1896 case of *Plessy v. Ferguson*. This was a civil case, used to justify the establishment of separate, segregated school systems. However, in 1954 the U.S. Supreme Court overturned *Plessy v. Ferguson*, thus beginning an era of federal intervention in American education. In the last two decades the Supreme Court, as well as countless lower federal courts, have ruled on a multitude of education-related issues. In doing so, the courts have greatly changed both the style and the direction of American education, arousing great debate as to the future of locally-controlled education. While each of the three branches of the federal government has authority and performs functions having direct bearing on the schools of our nation, public attention in recent years has been directed toward federal court decisions.

Most of the cases that have reached the United States Supreme Court pertain to the human rights sections of the Constitution, particularly those in the First and Fourteenth Amendments.[10] These have been of great importance in the various suits dealing with race and religion in the schools. Less often the Fifth Amendment, relating to self-incrimination, has been used in cases connected with allegedly subversive activities.

As written, the First Amendment prevented the federal government from interfering in human rights; however, the states could act as they desired in these matters. Only with the passing of the Fourteenth Amendment in 1868 were the federal courts permitted to intervene in the protection of basic civil rights as they pertained to citizens within the states. Although there has been an increased emphasis placed on human freedoms, it should be noted that during the period between 1789 and 1888 only three decisions relating to the public schools were handed down by the Supreme Court. During the period of 1889 to 1948 there were twenty-two renderings.

[9] C. Strough, "Long Hair and Short Tempers," *School Management* (18 June 1974), pp. 20-21.

[10] An important observation is that none of the cases focused directly upon the quality of education offered by the schools; only recently has anyone challenged through the courts the quality of education given to a child. A California mother brought a suit against the local school board because her son had graduated from high school with a fifth-grade reading competence.

With the accelerated controversy over human rights in recent years, the number of decisions handed down on schools has increased considerably.[11]

Rights of Schools

In the past fifteen years, the U.S. Supreme Court, as well as lower federal courts, have ruled on a wide variety of cases that affect the educational process from the time before the child arrives at the school door (busing) until the last activity of the day ends (sports and extracurricular activities). In doing so, the federal courts have changed the direction as well as the fabric of American education.

To say that federal court decisions on education have been controversial and, at times, divisive, is to be guilty of a gross understatement. Throughout the 1960's, the movements to impeach Justices Earl Warren and William Douglas were largely fueled by their voicing Supreme Court decisions on education (having the greatest effect in urban areas). Many conservatives who were not necessarily racists or pro-segregationists saw the Court decisions as federal interference in matters assigned by the Constitution to local governments. Those who were segregationists saw the rulings as a threat to their whole way of life; of course, they were. Most of those who opposed the federal court interventions, for whatever reason, cited fear that they would lead to the imposition of restrictions and rules which would curtail the freedom of action of local school districts. Ironically, as Pierson points out, the Supreme Court decisions tended to extend rights rather than limit them. What the Court did, in many instances, was to insist that students and teachers in public schools be guaranteed the same rights of religious freedom and due process as were other American citizens.[12]

Summerfield, while acknowledging that there had been increased federal interference in education, pointed out that the interventions had been effected to correct injustices and not to impose arbitrary regulations.[13] Naturally, the result has been to curb the authority of some school board members who have operated their districts as small fiefdoms, with little concern for quality or equality. Nolte, one of the most noted proponents of the rights and authority of local school boards, argued that each court

[11] Edward C. Bolmeier, *Landmark Supreme Court Decisions on Public School Issues* (Charlottesville, Va.: Michie, 1973), pp. 7-8.

[12] William L. Pierson, *Politics and Education* (Bloomington, Ind.: Phi Delta Kappa Educational Foundation, 1975), p. 14.

[13] H. L. Summerfield, *Power and Process* (Athens, Ga.: University of Georgia Press, 1974), pp. 229-231.

decision weakened and further eroded the power of local school boards to the extent that they have all the responsibilities with none of the powers.[14]

Free Speech. Court decisions such as the *Tinker* case have been disfavored by those who would like to preserve the authority and autonomy of the local school board. The case involved the suspension of students who wore black armbands during a one-day nationwide protest against the Vietnam War. The *Tinker* decision declared for the first time that children were "persons" under the Constitution, but more importantly, that they do not shed their constitutional rights at the schoolhouse gate. This case clearly set forth that due process must be afforded students. Nolte [15] pointed out that extending the rights of due process to all students has led to a heavy encroachment upon local board authority. For example, extending the right of freedom of speech to students has, in effect, resulted in the prohibition of local school boards to dismiss, suspend, or expel students for exercising such rights. In most cases, civil libertarians have hailed the dicisions as promoting individual liberties, while advocates of school board authority have viewed the decisions as a catalyst to erode local control. Other related court decisions have held that a teacher cannot be fired for expressing a political opinion in a situation in which such an opinion does not interfere with teaching performances.

These changes have caused endless debate not only about the role of education in the urban-metropolitan community, but in every American community: are we to educate children in the traditional manner, with the total emphasis on the three R's? Or is education a socializing and training situation in which the learning of social mores and political doctrines is as important as the three R's? Is the education of the next generation too important to be left in the hands of parents and amateurs who sit on school boards? Which is more important, to reflect the feelings and mores of the community or those of the nation? These questions, and the question of the abuse of local powers and authorities, have led to increased intervention by the federal courts. Hutchins has described the decisions of the court as fateful. They will affect not only the students of today, but the structure of society tomorrow.[16]

Desegregation. Race, too, has presented a challenge to the federal court system. The *Brown v. Board of Education* holding set the stage for the activist trend in desegreation of public schools. The *Brown* decision

[14] M. C. Nolte, "Supreme Court's New Rules for Due Process," *American School Board Journal* 162 (March 1975): 47-48.

[15] Ibid.

[16] R. M. Hutchins, "Two Fateful Decisions," *Education Digest* 40 (April 1975): 20.

caused the death of the old "separate-but-equal" principle set down in *Plessy v. Ferguson* and continued in the footsteps of the *Sweatt* [17] and *McLaurin* [18] cases, which had forecast the extension of desegregation from the college campus to the grade school. *Brown* expounded the principle that even when all tangible facilities were equal, the segregation of black children from white children in public schools still denied black children equal protection under the law as expressed in the Fourteenth Amendment. The *Brown* decision has led to numerous suits in the courts, both as defiance and as a means of seeking to expand the decision.

The busing of students to achieve racial balance in schools is but one of the ongoing aspects of desegregation rulings. This has often brought about violent reactions, notwithstanding the Court ruling handed down in *Swann* [19] which stated that busing is a legitimate instrument to eradicate the dual system swiftly and effectively. However, the Court clearly stated in *Swann* that if other methods could be discovered and implemented, then school districts would not necessarily have to resort to busing. Of course, busing has been used for years. Before *Brown,* for example, many black children were bused long distances past all-white schools. Yet many argue that transporting young children for long distances merely to achieve racial balance is a risk to the health of the children and impinges upon the educational process.

Responding to this issue, the Warren Court unanimously declared that separate education instilled in the black child a feeling of inferiority which affected the child's motivation to learn and which might affect his or her heart and mind in ways that could never be undone.[20] As a consequence of this response, during the past fifteen years the federal courts have taken the lead in promoting the process of desegregation. At first, court decisions and orders led to the desegregation of Southern public schools. In the past ten years the courts have focused their attention outside the South. Court decisions have led to busing orders in cities such as Detroit; Cleveland and Columbus, Ohio; and Boston.

---

[17] *Sweatt v. Painter* (1950), ruled that a Negro student had to be admitted to the University of Texas Law School because the alternate school for Negro students was not equal.

[18] *McLaurin v. Oklahoma State Regents for Higher Education* (1950) ruled that a black student admitted to the University of Oklahoma had to receive treatment equal to that of white students (no separate tables in the dining room or separate seating in class).

[19] *Swann v. Charlotte-Mecklenburg Board of Education* (1971) ruled that schools had to adopt segregation plans that worked immediately, instead of proceeding at their own speed. If not, the court would dispatch an expert and implement the expert's plan.

[20] Henry J. Abraham, *Freedom and the Court* (New York: Oxford University Press, 1972), pp. 313-315.

Although a federal district court in 1976 found Cleveland guilty of intentional segregation in its schools, it took the Cleveland school board until 1979 to implement a court-ordered desegregation program. The ruling, however, has been appealed to the United States Supreme Court by the city's school board. The school board is also watching a suit pending in the federal court in Cincinnati. The suit alleges complicity in the Cincinnati public schools because of their racial imbalance in more than twelve predominantly white schools. If the ruling goes against the school board, it could force Cincinnati into a city-suburban desegregation program and have a great impact on a number of other metropolitan city-suburban areas.

In Louisville, Kentucky, and Wilmington, Delaware,[21] and other areas, the courts have moved against *de facto* segregation and have ordered busing between the largely black inner cities and the largely white suburbs. These decisions have received violent reaction from many of the white middle and upper-middle classes. To them, such decisions seem to strike at the fabric of American society by negating the right of average (white middle- and upper-class) citizens to move and live (segregated) where they feel their children will receive the best education. To inner-city parents, these decisions seem the only way to ensure the end of segregation and to obtain quality education for their children. To others they seem to represent an extension of the federal government into local affairs while some feel that the end is worth the means but are troubled by the violent reactions.[22]

There is yet another viewpoint. Many inner-city parents are as adamantly against busing as are parents in the largely white suburbs—including middle–class Blacks—albeit for different reasons. These parents represent the disenchanted: those who have grown increasingly skeptical regarding the advantages of the racially mixed student and teacher populations in view of the lack of dramatic changes in academic achievement; those equally disturbed by the one-way, black-to-white school busing situations, which place the onus of integration on black families; and those disturbed by the fact that black students have no true affiliation with or participatory membership in their schools' activities, particularly after-school events unavoidably scheduled at times when they are enroute home.

While the Supreme Court might well be the leader and conscience of the land, the purse and sword are still in the other branches of the govern-

---

[21] Wilmington, Delaware, is the first metropolitan school district to cross district lines with a desegregation plan. The success or failure of the Wilmington plan will probably determine the fate of desegregation.

[22] To this author, busing students is not the answer to quality education. It still leaves the inner-city schools without competent teachers or appropriate resources. A student should be guaranteed a quality education regardless of his or her place of residence.

ment. In the *Holmes County* case of 1969, the Court stated that striving to attain desegregation at all deliberate speed was no longer Constitutionally permissible, and ordered school districts to end dual school systems at once. But even in good faith, how much busing will the Constitution require to achieve this ideal one-school system? That is, how much, how far, and at what cost? Racial quotas and the pairing or grouping of schools are other methods suggested as devices to remove all traces of state-imposed segregation. What about neighborhood housing patterns in Northern cities and their suburbs? The Court gave federal district judges broad powers to use racial quotas in fashioning desegregation plans. The majority of Americans have always favored the neighborhood school concept, and the Court admitted that, all else being equal, it was desirable to assign pupils to the school nearest to their homes; but since things were far from equal, it was obvious to the courts that busing would be necessary to create racially integrated schools.

School Finance. School finance has proved to be as important an issue as desegregation, with the potential of affecting every school child. Several lower court decisions have struck at the root of local support and control of education. The question of school finance is a difficult one, as discussed in Chapter Four. Currently, the federal courts are looking at the constitutionality of the local property tax as a source of school revenue. Public attention was first drawn to this issue in the cases of *Serrano v. Priest* and *San Antonio Independent School District v. Rodriguez*. In both of these cases the court held that public-school financing that relies mainly on local property tax for funding the school system causes great disparities in the amount of revenue expended for individual students. This has been held to discriminate against the poor child. The right to an education in the public-school system should not be conditioned upon the wealth of a child's parents and neighbors. Affluent districts can provide a higher quality of education for their children, given the present method for financing. The courts have held that this denies the plaintiffs equal protection under the Fourteenth Amendment. Court decisions surrounding this issue have begun to have a tremendous impact in all states which rely upon the local property tax as the chief source of school revenue, and are forcing states to seriously look for other ways to provide a more equitable system for generating funds to operate the schools.[23]

Only the case of *San Antonio Independent School District v. Rodriguez* has reached the Supreme Court. In this case, decided in 1973, the Court ruled on narrow grounds for the district. However, in doing so, the Court

----

[23] John E. Coons, "Financing Public Schools After Rodriguez," *Saturday Review-World* 1 (9 October 1977): 44-47.

ruling established guidelines for future rulings. By ruling that the state had provided for a certain level of equality by establishing a basic level of support for all districts to ensure a minimum level of equality, the Court established the fact that there must be a basic level of support for all students. This action has upset the traditional local support of schools and replaced it with state support. It also called for an entirely new financing system. This has been denounced by some as further interference with the local area's right to support education so far as it can. Several similar cases are being reviewed in lower courts.

Religion. Many school cases have developed over religious questions. The First Amendment, applicable to the states by virtue of the Fourteenth Amendment, states that Congress shall make no law respecting the establishment of religion or barring the free exercise of such. The relationship between religion and education affects individuals' most cherished values and beliefs. Basically, there are four cases of conflict concerning the relationship between schools and religion. One concerns the spending of public tax money for what may be termed a religious purpose. A second instance is the inclusion in public schools of activities that may be deemed to hold religious connotations. A third problem has arisen when public schools have required participation in activities which are contrary to the religious convictions of certain pupils. A fourth issue involves the right of the state to regulate the concerns of non-public schools operated and financed by religious organizations.[24]

May tax money from the public be expended for religious purposes? According to *Cochran v. Louisiana State Board of Education,* the answer to this question is yes. This issue questioned the constitutionality of a Louisiana law which authorized public funds to be used to provide textbooks, free of charge, to non-public school students. The State Board of Education, being governed by the legislation, allocated funds to all students regardless of whether they attended public or non-public schools. Grieved by this action, a group of citizens brought suit to restrain the practice, charging that the use of public funds for private purposes was in violation of the Fourteenth Amendment. The Court held that there was no constitutional objection to a state issuing secular textbooks to non-public school students. This was the beginning of the "child benefit theory": that public funds may be allocated to all schools, public or private, if these expenditures will benefit the student.

The second category concerns religious activities permissible in the public school. This issue was decided by the Supreme Court in two key

[24] Sam Duker, *The Public Schools and Religion: The Legal Context* (New York: Harper and Row, 1966), pp. 21-22.

cases, *Schempp v. School District of Abington Township* and *Engel v. Vitale.* In *Engel v. Vitale,* the issue involved New York State school officials who had composed a prayer and required it to be recited each day in the classroom. A group of parents brought suit, charging that such a prayer requirement violated the First Amendment and was contrary to their own beliefs and those of their children. The Court held that the requirement of a state-composed prayer violated the Establishment Clause of the First Amendment.

The *Schempp* case challenged the constitutionality of mandated Bible reading in the public schools. The parents of the Schempp children brought suit against the State of Pennsylvania, charging a violation of their First Amendment rights through the Fourteenth Amendment. The court concurred, citing not only the Establishment Clause but also the fact that the reading of the Bible implies a preference of one corpus of religious thought over others. The Court seems to have left room for Bible study in public education. However, the problem for school authorities is to distinguish what is or is not permissible under the First Amendment, and how far they can go in the teaching of religion.[25]

The third type of conflict regards the question of classroom activities from which a student may be excused because of religious beliefs. One such Supreme Court case, *West Virginia State Board of Education v. Barnette,* challenged the state's right to require students to salute the flag in the classroom. A group of Jehovah's Witnesses charged that the requirement was contrary to their religious beliefs. The Court ruled against the requirement, stating that the right to differ by refusing to stand and participate in the flag salute may not be withheld.

The fourth category bears upon parochial schools. *Pierce v. Society of Sisters* remains the classic precedent in this area. In this case, the Court held that a state may not force a child to attend a public school rather than a private, parochial one. It did not, however, free non-public schools from adhering to the same standards imposed on the public schools.

---

[25] A prominent case which ultimately was brought before the United States Supreme Court for final disposal, *Doremus v. Board of Education* (1950), typifies the early stage of judicial reaction to litigation regarding the legality of Bible reading in the public schools. Here certain parents brought action against the school board and the state to test the constitutionality of a statute which provided that five verses from the Bible be read in class. The state court ruled against the parents, and the United States Supreme Court dismissed the case for want of jurisdiction which, in effect, let the state court decision stand. Thirteen years later, the United States Supreme Court heard an almost identical case arising from a Pennsylvania Bible reading requirement statute, and this time the Court ruled the law unconstitutional (*Abington School District v. Schempp,* 1963).

If the *Pierce* court had ruled in favor of the state, it would have marked the end of private school systems. Those supporting the right of the state to impose public school attendance contended that there was ample time for supplementary religious education to be offered after regular school hours. It was the belief of the court that such a procedure would deprive citizens of their rights of liberty and property without due process of law and equal protection as guaranteed by the Fourteenth Amendment.

In retrospect, it is not surprising that the Supreme Court stirs controversy whenever it rules in cases dealing with religion in the schools.[26] In these legal actions, a minority group is seeking to gain protection of its constitutional rights. Naturally, the majority is frequently pained when its values seem to be disregarded by the Court. In cases which have revolved around religion in the schools, one or more members of the Court have held a view contrary to that of the majority.[27]

Curriculum. Early court cases indicate that state judiciaries followed rather closely the old common law whereby the parents rule supreme over the child during the child's minority. In *School Board District No. 18 v. Thompson,* a 1909 Oklahoma case, the parents refused to allow their children to take singing lessons and the children were expelled from school. Ruling in favor of the parents, the court stated: "To our mind, the right of the Board of Education to prescribe the course of study and to designate the text-books to be used does not carry with it the absolute power to require the pupils to study all of the branches prescribed in the course in opposition to the parents' reasonable wishes in relation to some of them."[28]

Some decades ago parents began to object to inclusions in the curriculum of knowledge other than "book learning." In *Hardwick v. Board of Trustees,* a California court in 1921 ruled that the school had a right to compel a student to take part in dancing as part of the curriculum, even though she considered the costumes worn in the class to be indecent and sinful because they were so brief. She was allowed to wear anything she chose to the class, but her father objected on the grounds that dressing differently would subject the girl to ridicule. The court ruled that the girl

---

[26] In cases dealing with the Establishment Clause, it is apparent that the Court feels there is a "wall of separation" between the church and the state. It is not likely that the Court will retreat from this view in the near future. There is a great deal of public opposition to the *Engel* and *Schempp* rulings, since many feel that America is a "godly" country and must remain so, and that the Bible must not be driven from the schoolroom. Those holding this view feel that the Constitution should be amended to nullify the ourt rulings in these cases.

[27] Duker, pp. 44-47.

[28] *School Board District No. 18 v. Thompson,* 24 Okla. 1, 103P, 578 (1909).

must attend and maintained that the requirement did not violate her constitutional rights.

Sex Education. A controversial issue during the last decade has been sex education. A 1970 Kansas case on the subject is *TASTE, Inc. v. Topeka Board of Education.* The suit was brought against the school board by TASTE, Inc., a Topeka organization which held that sex education taught in the schools was unconstitutional for several reasons: it violates Article 1 of the Fourteenth Amendment "because it destroys our personal and inalienable rights to liberty and happiness in that it is designed to question parental authority by encouraging analysis, appraisal and criticism of parental authority," and that parents have a right to have children not taught subjects which are "repugnant to the family." In addition, this organization also felt that the teaching of sex is contrary to the Ninth and Tenth Amendments.

Implications

It is obvious that the federal court system will continue to play an important role in public education. The abuses by local boards over the past years have ensured that there will be a need for future court decisions. More importantly, education has become so expensive and so complex that, as more than one expert has put it, it should not be left to parents and other amateurs. Local school districts are no longer able to provide for all the needs of all the students. The great disparity in standards of education, once considered a local prerogative, is no longer tolerated. With the homogenization of the American society have come demands for the homogenization of the educational process. Our knowledge of the sociology of knowledge and of its effects upon the child and upon society were not dreamed of two hundred years ago. As education grows increasingly important, it is perceived that local control is not as advantageous as it was once thought to be.

There are several factors which have contributed to the composition of the school board, not the least of which has been the fact that the amount of time needed to serve has practically eliminated the lower and middle classes from representation. Factory workers and farmers rarely can take time off in the middle of the day for luncheon conferences. Thus, membership has fallen to the older, wealthier, and more conservative members of the community. To many, this type of board has seemed unresponsive to community needs, forcing the community to turn to the courts for redress of their grievances.

Not all the effects of federal court decisions have been felt yet. These decisions tend to have ripple effects. For example, the *Rodriguez* decision, although ostensibly in favor of local and state school boards, has forced most states to re-examine their school finance systems.[29] This may be, in the long run, the most important court decision since *Brown v. Board of Education*. If a revision of school financing systems can lead to better education, it will certainly further diminish local control.

Other decisions in the area of due process have had a deterrent effect. School boards are not taking actions which they routinely took in this area just twenty years ago. While it would be premature to say that all students and teachers are being granted full rights, there is a tendency for school boards to be overtolerant, resulting in lower quality education for students. Although federal courts are sure to continue to press for integration, they may soften their position on the issue of busing as it becomes apparent that busing is not solving the problem for which it was intended.

Part of the problem with the educational system and the role of the courts is that nowhere in the body of the Constitution, or in any of its amendments, is education mentioned; therefore, most cases reflect a concept of education which is derived from interpretations of the First and Fourteenth Amendments. Unless this is changed there will be a continuation of problems, suits, and clarifications, with the decisions of the courts reflecting changing mores and times. It is apparent that federal intervention has become an integral part of the American educational system because state and local districts have failed to carry out their Constitutional responsibility to all people. There is no evidence in sight to suggest that there will be any less intervention in the years to come. Education has become big business, and the federal government specializes in big business. Now let us turn to a much lower level of the political process—local politics and its effects on educational processes.

Local Politics

Wayne Chesing, a developmental psychologist, once claimed that schools only reflect those values for which society and parents have a deep respect or which they hold sacred, and that we must change society in order to change the schools. If this is true, then educators should pack up and go home.

The underlying assumption is that politics governs our educational system. If we allow for a modification of the political process such that the

[29] The rippling effect of California's Proposition 13 is causing many states to re-examine their school finance systems.

total urban community becomes a vital part of it, then we will not only change the schools, but we will change society to reflect our educational system rather than have the school system reflect a battered and confused society. In order to develop this assumption, there is a necessary awareness that must be reached. The total urban community must first realize that politics does govern the education of its children. Politicians decide how money will be raised—through increases in local real estate taxes or greater appropriations from the state. Politicians provide the answers to certain questions: How is the money to be distributed among the schools? Who should decide the type of resources to be purchased? What schools will receive these resources? From whom should the district buy its resources? What are the rights of students and parents? What are the criteria for teacher selection? Who should decide the salaries and benefits for administrators and teachers? Who should resolve the school building program? Who should determine the school district boundaries? There are many more areas that are affected by the political process. We are going to look at a few of these areas and attempt to show how they directly affect the education of the urban child.

A political system generally is manipulated by many different groups of people. Usually each of these groups has a specific interest. The groups exerting the most power will ordinarily have the greatest influence on the system. Sometimes two or more groups join together because of a common interest in order to develop a broader power base with which to negotiate this interest. Thus, urban parents must realize that it is necessary to initiate the group process in order to have a significant impact on the political process that directly influences the education of their children.

Group process and power is exemplified by teacher unions. Given a choice between supporting teachers, students, or parents, most school officials have no problem deciding whom to support—they will support the most strongly organized group. In urban areas this group is usually the teachers' union.

What are some of the major authorities affecting the education of the urban child and how do they operate within the political system? That is, how is the game of politics played?

Politics and the School Board

In many urban areas, school board trustees are publicly-elected officials; in other cities they are appointed by the mayor. Theoretically, if the board of trustees is elected, the citizens have a voice in the political process that governs the educational system. In reality, this is not true because citizens have not learned how to hold public officials accountable.[30] When the school board is appointed by the mayor, the board will often function as a group politically organized to negotiate the interests and concerns of the mayor and not the concerns of parents and the interests of students. In fact, most appointments to the school board are political payments by the mayor to individuals or groups of individuals for favors; consequently, these school board appointments have very little to do with qualifications or with a real interest in the education of children. In this way men and women are placed in positions with the authority to vote away millions of tax dollars each year without full knowledge of how their actions benefit the educational process.[31]

The political tool used by the school board to keep parents and concerned citizens ignorant of how the school system is actually run is the executive session. The executive session is an effective mechanism to protect many administrators and teachers from being held accountable to the citizenry. If parents and other citizens were made aware of the many administrative malpractices that occur each year, they would demand that the school board release its incompetent administrators and teachers. Undoubtedly, this would cause serious confrontations between the boards and the unions, and the boards are not about to provoke strong teachers' unions if they can avoid it. The executive session has become a way to keep parents at arm's length from the real factors that are preventing their children from receiving an adequate education, and there is no practical method to dispose of it. The Sunshine Law, created to eradicate this problem, requires school boards to have open meetings. This law is

[30] The urban poor have learned how to very effectively elect people to office. But they have not learned how to hold them accountable. The reason is simple enough: after their candidate is elected, they return home and wait for the changes to take place. The most effective way to hold elected officials accountable is to work with the officials to bring about the changes. In this way, the people will know if the official is making every effort to bring about change. If she or he is not bringing about the expected changes, the populace will be close enough to the problem to identify incompetencies.

Many times, because of the distance between the people and the elected official, what appears to be incompetence is, in actuality, the result of a lack of sufficient resources to bring about effective change. In other cases, it is attributed to irresponsiveness.

[31] It is uncertain whether those responsible for the school curriculum know what kind of resources are needed to effect a thorough and efficient educational system. A reflection of that obscurity is the issue of objectivity with full knowledge, as opposed to objectivity without full knowledge. Whereas there are no preparatory restrictions for school board memberships, medical and legal board memberships are restricted to *only* those who have exhibited outstanding leadership in their fields of medicine and jurisprudence, respectively.

meaningless; when parents demand its enforcement, the board meets in even greater secrecy.

A more structured type of political maneuvering takes place when school district boundaries are being established. This maneuver is called gerrymandering, a situation in which district boundaries are set by the school board in response to the pressures and demands of a group of organized citizens. Gerrymandering often results in having a student who lives across the street from a school denied admission because he lives outside of the school's district. Why? Because the district happens to end at his street. If the zoning had been done correctly, the school would be in the center of the school district. Historically, school districts have been zoned to keep Blacks and other minorities out of certain schools; today some form of gerrymandering is still used to regulate student admissions, and we still find quasi-private schools within many urban school districts.

The move toward desegregation is another good example of how school boards respond to organized groups. In large urban cities such as Boston, Louisville, Wilmington, Cleveland, and many others in the North and South, school boards have inspired the opposition against court desegregation plans that mandated busing by their unwillingness to cooperate with the courts. In the case of integration, school boards have received most of their pressure from groups opposed to busing who proclaim, "We do not want to bus our children too far away from home." But, according to Julian Bond, it is not the bus that's the problem, it's where the bus is bound. Dick Gregory claimed that if the school board had told the parents of South Boston that their children were going to be bused to a school where they would sit with sons and daughters of Rockefellers and DuPonts, those parents would have helped to drive the buses. Political pressures have caused many school boards to participate in politically organized moves which have resulted in the failure to carry out federal court orders to desegregate.

One of the most crucial responsibilities that lies within the jurisdiction of the school board is the distribution of resources. If one school district seems to be better equipped than another to offer quality education to its pupils, then it is obvious that the school board is favoring one school district over the other when it distributes its resources. As long as there are selective schools, such as comprehensive or academic preparatory schools, there will always be an uneven distribution of resources.[32] The

[32] Many selective public schools have enormous resources supplied by donors. These donors have always existed in the upper-class white community. The black bourgeoisie has not taken financial interest in the public schools; its members prefer to send their children to private schools. In most metropolitan areas there are enough middle- and upper-middle-class blacks to determine whether or not the schools in their district will have adequate financial resources.

existence of selective schools encourages some schools to be better than others. The identification of certain schools as nonacademic institutions encourages teachers in these schools not to teach and students not to learn. Good teachers and administrators are prompted to go to the better schools, leaving the disadvantaged students with the underdeveloped and incompetent teachers and administrators.

Selective schools, as well as the distinction between public and private schools, have created the kind of society we now have. As warm and cold air causes storms, different values and lifestyles cause violence and turbulence. Both selective and private schools abet the concept of "separate but equal." Equality will never become a reality as long as public school students are not given the same degree of protection from crime and corruption as that given to private and selective school students.

In spite of these obstructions, it is not impossible to make the school board accountable. If the board is elected, then parents should organize themselves in order to get control of that election process. If the school board is appointed by the mayor, then parents should consider confronting the mayor and demanding that he support their concerns. After all, the mayor is elected by the people. In either case, parents and concerned citizens should be politically astute and well-organized if they expect to gain accountability from those who are officially responsible for their children's education.

Politics and Teachers' Unions

If you do not belong to the group that the union represents, then you should not expect to profit from it. It is important for the urban community and, in particular, for parents to fully understand the concept and implications of unionism. Parents need to understand that unionism can and will work against them and against the interests of their children. It can work for them only if they become part of a strong, organized group or union of their own with the power to arbitrate with school boards in the same manner as do teachers' unions.

Teachers' unions are composed of large groups of teachers, politically organized to negotiate the interests of teachers, not the interests of students. Administrators' unions consist of large groups of administrators, politically organized to negotiate the interests of administrators.

It is not difficult to determine how such organizations gain political support. The *New York Times* reported that the American Federation of Teachers in the state of New York loaned $150 million to New York City to help keep the city from going into default.[33] This money came from

[33] These loans were made through the purchase of municipal bonds.

retirement benefits for teachers, tax dollars paid toward the teachers' fringe benefits. Who gets the support of the New York City officials on matters regarding educational policies, the school teachers or the parents? In 1975, the National Education Association was listed as contributing $2.5 million to candidates for congressional and state offices through its state and local affiliates. It was reported that, in New York City alone, $1 million was given to support political candidates. The teachers' unions backed 147 candidates and had 133 victories. Who controls urban education in New York City? Is it surprising that court injunctions against strikes are reluctantly and weakly enforced?

Which group of lobbyists applied the greatest pressure upon Congress to pass the bill for a new Department of Education, the National Education Association, a national parents' association, or a national students' association? Who will have the greatest influence on the new departments?

Teachers' unions have lobbyists in state capitals and in Washington, D.C., to help assure better conditions for teachers; however, with the exception of a request for smaller classroom size, parents will find few, if any, clauses in any teachers' union contract calling for better education for students. These arguments are not intended to advocate the suspension of teachers' unions, but rather to illustrate that teachers' unions have great political influence on the urban child's education.

Politics and the Superintendent

Regarding tenure, it makes little difference whether teachers and administrators are good, bad, or average—if they have tenure they will be employed for another decade or two. It is uncommon to hear of a superintendent dismissing a teacher or an administrator for incompetence, even though there are increasing numbers of English teachers hired by urban schools who cannot pass a tenth-grade composition examination, and a large number of mathematics teachers hired who cannot perform above the 60 percent performance level of a twelfth-grade mathematics competency examination.[34] Occasionally a superintendent will remove a

---

[34] I have served as a mathematics test consultant for three large urban school districts. In one, the examination given to teachers was equivalent to a twelfth-grade mathematics achievement test. The district required that a person applying for a teaching position in secondary mathematics correctly answer thirty-six items out of a total of sixty—a 60 percent performance level. The other two districts' requirements were not much better.

The rationale for not having higher requirements was that these teachers would only be teaching in a junior high school. There are two important questions to be considered: (1) Should they be teaching in a junior high school? (2) What would keep them from moving on to a senior high school if a vacancy were to occur and they

principal from a school because of his inability to run the school effectively, but will then place him in a principalship in another school across town or in a position in the central administration with equivalent status and salary.[35]

Developmental theory informs us that by the time the average child is ten years of age he or she will have passed through the first three stages of development (pre-occupational, occupational, and concrete). This should be a signal to superintendents that the primary grades are the most important years of a child's educational development. Edmund Gordon, an educational psychologist at Yale University, headed a team of consultants for the Philadelphia School Board of Trustees in 1974. The team was asked to conduct a study and to make recommendations as to where the board should focus its Title I funds. The consultants recommended that Title I funds be put in the primary grades, K-3. Their findings suggested that students who were exposed to the best of what the educational system had to offer during these crucial years would be able to educationally advance in subsequent years in spite of the system.

It is hard to believe that superintendents remain unaware of this phenomenon, yet their techniques for the selection and retention of teachers are the same for the primary grades as they are for all other grades.

There is no doubt that superintendents would like to free their school systems of these incompetents, but they realize that it would result in serious confrontations with the unions. This is especially true if the board members are elected and cannot afford to become political enemies of teachers' unions. On the other hand, if the board members are appointed by the mayor, pressure comes from the mayor since teachers' unions have financial investments in the election process.

Political pressures such as these cause many superintendents to play it safe. They continue to build mediocrity and incompetence into the educational system at the cost of quality education. Politically, it is less embarrassing and less threatening for a superintendent to shift the mediocrity and incompetence around within the system than to free the system of such ineptitude. Meanwhile, underdeveloped schools remain the same or get worse, and the unsolved problems are ignored and become more serious.

---

had seniority? These same teachers would be denied permission to teach in the suburban schools within the same school districts.

[35] An enormous waste of money results because school districts choose not to relieve themselves of their incompetent employees. Most of the paralysis is due to a fear of unions. Staggering wastes of human resources occur when positions are created for incompetent teachers and administrators; this, in part, results in a surplus of administrators in the urban school districts.

Nevertheless, the superintendent is the chief academician and administrator of the school system. Most citizens believe that the superintendent should be a man or woman of integrity. Unfortunately, integrity is very seldom rewarded in an urban school system. Experience shows that a superintendent guided by integrity will not last two years unless, of course, he or she has the full support of the parents, the courts, and the school board. No urban-area superintendent gets this kind of support; therefore, she or he will continue to "play politics" like any other successful politician. In this case, the game is played with the urban child's education and future.

Politics and Parents

For years the American Federation of Teachers (AFT) and the National Education Association (NEA) were separate and rival teachers' organizations. The AFT was looked upon more as a bargaining union than as a professional association. The NEA was perceived as more of a professional association opposed to such concepts as teacher strikes.

The rivalry between the two organizations began to create a problem for both groups. Many of the NEA members began to shift their membership to the AFT because they believed the latter to be more effective in representing the local interests of teachers. Other teachers could not financially afford membership in both organizations and had to choose between the two. For years each organization struggled to gain power over the other. When both realized that as long as they opposed each other neither would have the power to represent the teachers' interests effectively, they began to negotiate ways to attain peaceful coexistence. Parents must realize that there is little room for more than one representative parents' organization in a school district. Two or more only abates the kind of power and influence that parents can exert on behalf of their children's education.

As an illustration, a school board in a large urban community was deliberating the question of whether school counselors should have the right to withhold from parents confidential information (concerning venereal disease, pregnancy, etc.) about their children. One parental organization voted "yes" to the question, and the other organization in the same district voted "no." The conflict between the two organizations left the school board free to act, uninfluenced by either group. Often when there are two parental organizations, only one is recognized by the board. In order to constitute a viable force, parents must put forth a total effort through one organization. They must not allow their children to be the victims of the power play that often takes place between different parent organizations.

In this chapter we have attempted to show that our system of education is greatly influenced by a high degree of structural politics. The challenge facing urban educators is that they must develop an educational system that will coexist with the political system. The kind of educational system needed to accomplish this is one that utilizes every available resource within the community, one in which the city becomes a living curriculum. This may be the only viable approach to take if public schools are to survive.

Citations

Alexander et al. v. Holmes County Board of Education et al., 396 U.S. 802 (1969).

Brown v. Board of Education, 347 U.S. 483, 74 Sup. Ct. 686 (1954).

Cochran v. Louisiana State Board of Education, 281 U.S. 370, 50 Sup. Ct. 335 (1930).

Doremus v. Board of Education, 5 N.J. 435, 75 A. 2d 880 (1950).

Engle v. Vitale, 370 U.S. 421, 82 Sup. Ct. 1261 (1962).

Hardwick v. Board of Trustees, 54 Cal. App. 696, 205 49 (1921).

McLaurin v. Oklahoma State Regents for Higher Education, 339 U.S. 637 (1950).

Pierce v. Society of Sisters, 286 U.S. 510, 45 Sup. Ct. 571 (1925).

Plessy v. Ferguson, 161 U.S. 537 (1895).

San Antonio Independent School District v. Rodriguez, 411 U.S. 1 (1973).

Schempp v. School District of Abington Township, 374 U.S. 203, 83 Sup. Ct. 1560 (1963).

School Board District No. 18 v. Thompson, 24 Okla. 1, 103P 578 (1909).

Serrano v. Priest, 487 P. 2d 1241 (1971).

Swann v. Charlotte-Mecklenburg Board of Education, 402 U.S. 1 (1971).

Sweatt v. Painter, 339 U.S. 629 (1950).

TASTE Inc. v. Topeka Board of Education, Ks. (1970). From Naples notes.

Tinker v. DesMoines Independent Community School District, 393 U.S. 503 (1969).

West Virginia State Board of Education v. Barnette, 319 U.S. 624, 63 Sup. Ct. 1178 (1943).

6

Techniques and Recommendations for Change

Claude Mayberry, Jr.

Despite the extensive research already undertaken, the solutions to problems in education faced by the urban population are by no means clear. One factor that has contributed to this confusion has been the failure of cities systematically to use all their available resources to analyze and build upon their existing knowledge. Often, this has led the educational community to weak or inadequate conceptual bases for educational development and, therefore, to contravene the development of human resources.

Although student discipline is a major problem in the urban schools, no techniques are offered to change this condition. This omission is by design and not by oversight. If the total urban community serves as the foundation for the school curriculum, if teachers and staff raise their expectations and standards for their students, and if the school board of trustees raises its expectations and standards for teachers and administrators, then the student disciplinary problem will no longer be the primary crisis in our urban schools.

This chapter offers techniques and recommendations that urban school district administrators can use in confronting the problems within their school districts in an efficient and cost-effective manner.

A Model Institute for Urban Education and Human Resource Development

For the past century, local governments and school districts (henceforth referred to as the *civil city* and the *school city,* respectively) have maintained their autonomy in order to assure their constituents that politics would not interfere with the educational process. In reality, this is nonsense. Nevertheless, these two corporate structures have always competed against each other for the same resources, sometimes consciously and at other times inadvertently. The model institute proposed here is an agency

106

developed to use the resources of both the civil city and the school city, and structured to specialize in curriculum and teaching, research and human development. The agency would also institute training and service programs designed to improve education within the legal corporate boundaries of the civil city within which the school city lies. This concept may also include two or three adjacent cities and their school districts, whose resources would be combined through a common institute.

The Institute should be structured in such a way that it will draw upon the staff and supportive resources of the civil city and school city administrations and, in addition, will seek to attract behavioral scientists to the study of urban education and child development within the structure of a well-defined teaching, learning, and development process. Since both corporate structures already have extensive programs focusing on human growth and development, the Institute will coordinate and expand these efforts. Its central purpose will be to help both administrations develop their own human resources by systematically attacking the problems of their underdeveloped populations.

During the initial stages, the Institute's staff should devote its attention to the tasks of rethinking identified problems and charting strategies for solutions. Particular attention should be given to the wide range of factors that influence educational success and failure within the educational process. The Institute should attend to such problems as the diversity and mobility of the population and the rigidity of systems by which the populace is served. It should give particular attention to the alternatives and techniques advocated in this book.

The primary objectives of the Institute for Urban Education and Human Resource Development should include: (1) developing conceptual bases and strategies from the ever-changing bodies of knowledge, research, and practice; (2) translating these concepts into competencies and skills which can be applied, within the school district, to the appraisal and enhancement of the developmental process; (3) applying these concepts to the development of educational materials and techniques, assessment instruments, and implementation procedures, and models and programs for a more effective education for the urban population; and, (4) teacher training and human resource development.

In order to minimize the political pressure that is likely to be exerted on an institute of this nature, the appointment of the director should be the responsibility of both the mayor of the city and the school board of trustees. In addition, the appointment should be approved by two-thirds of the city council. It is vital that the director have a political base if the Institute is to effect change.

There should be an advisory board or steering committee to assist the director. This board or committee should include at least the following representatives: officials from the offices of the mayor and the superintendent of schools, the teachers' union, and the parents' organization, as well as representatives from the city council, each court, major industries and businesses, the local Jaycees, the district congressional office, the district state representative and senate offices, and the local newspaper, plus one or two articulate parents, and spokespersons from additional community organizations as deemed necessary. One should not be concerned about the size of the committee; its primary purpose is to have input from the total community. The Institute staff should be capable of processing the volume of information flowing from the committee.

With this kind of representation and input, the city can become a living curriculum. If the urban community accepts this challenge it will be able to develop and coordinate a series of educational programs toward this end. The following are some examples of the kinds of programs that can be implemented through the Institute.

Legal Education

For years school teachers were proud to admit that they did not take part in politics. Although they were dissatisfied with the manner in which they were treated, they left politics to union officials. It is no surprise that their students remained complacent about politics and unaware of how it could alter their daily lives. Today school personnel have become more politically involved, albeit to serve their own self-interests. They have not incorporated meaningful politics into the curriculum. If we expect urban students to avoid becoming victims of the political process, we must begin to make the political and legal processes an integral part of the school curriculum.

As we examine the complexities of urbanization, it becomes evident that legal skills are necessary for a student to maximize his or her opportunity in a highly technical society. Legal language has become highly technical. It is unspoken and unwritten by most of the people in our society. Those who have mastered the language have tremendous power and influence over our lives. Because of this potential for power, it is crucial that urban school administrators consider incorporating legal language into their curriculum. It is the urban student who is most likely to become a victim of the legal system. Serious consideration must be given to the sophistication of the content and language used at each grade level to help students become acquainted with both the legal process and its language by the time they have completed their high school education.

The judicial branches of government in the city should be encouraged to cooperate with the Institute and assist in the establishment of a legal-educational program in the elementary and secondary grades. Through mutual cooperation of the Institute and officials of the court, legal agencies, and attorneys, funds could be raised from outside sources such as foundations, and state and federal governments. These funds would finance law students studying at nearby law schools to help the school district develop a legal education curriculum. Part-time assistants could be used throughout the year, just as courts and legal agencies for years have employed part-time law students to perform services. Financial aid in the form of work/study assistance can be given directly to college students during the summer, or during the academic year if the students are studying near an urban school district, to work on the development of a legal education curriculum.

Programs involving law enforcement agencies should also be integrated into the curriculum. It is not enough to have a speech given in the school once or twice a year: law enforcers such as city policemen and juvenile court personnel should become an inherent part of the school program. A long-range law enforcement program may reduce the high degree of corruption we are now witnessing in our law enforcement agencies. The city council and mayor should work closely with and assist the Institute in developing law enforcement programs that can be integrated into the school curriculum. If we can incorporate ROTC's into the curriculum to assist our armed forces, then we should be able to develop city ROTC's as a form of basic training for entry into our cities' law enforcement agencies.

Health Education

Everything written about the legal process and its incorporation into the school curriculum should apply equally to the medical process. No student should complete high school without a thorough understanding of the nature and functions of his or her own body. Students should have the knowledge of paramedical professionals by the time they graduate from high school. Medical practice as we know it in this country is the treatment of illness. Educators concerned with the concept of preventive medicine could eliminate much of the need for medical doctors as their role is currently defined through a comprehensive K-12 program.

If medical and dental agencies as well as dentists and physicians practicing in the urban community were to be encouraged to cooperate with the Institute, a comprehensive health education curriculum could be developed within the K-12 curriculum with the assistance of medical and paramedical students studying at nearby schools. Health-care programs could begin in the kindergarten: dentists could assist the Institute by promoting preventive dental care in the early primary grades; toothbrushes, toothpaste and dental floss could form a part of classroom supplies. Started during the first four years of school (K-3), good dental-health practices will become part of students' permanent behavior. Students should not only be instructed about oral hygiene, but should be given a chance each day to care for their teeth under the supervision of a teacher. Initially, a dentist could be invited to the classroom to demonstrate the use of the toothbrush and dental floss.[1] Administrators should explore the possibility of receiving donations of dental and medical supplies appropriate to the curriculum, or of purchasing them at a discount. The development of a dental-care program for the schools should be a function of the Institute.

There are numerous other creative ways to incorporate health education into the total curriculum. Beginning in elementary schools and continuing throughout the students' public school life, medical laboratories should be at their disposal—not for the purpose of developing doctors, but to teach students about the functions of their bodies and the maintenance of good health.[2] In the early grades, students should be instructed in the use of such instruments as a thermometer, a blood-pressure unit, and a stethoscope. Eventually, their vocabulary should include enough Latin to enable them to use a pharmaceutical dictionary. The Institute could develop a monthly medical journal for its students at all grade levels. This kind of curriculum would eventually encourage every family to own these and other instruments and materials necessary to monitor and maintain good health. The mayor and city council should assist the school district, through the Institute, to find financial aid to properly equip economically disadvantaged homes.

The lives of thousands of heart attack victims could be saved each year if victims were to receive cardiopulmonary resuscitation (CPR) immediately. Since hypertension is proportionally higher among Blacks, urban school administrators should consider CPR as a certification requirement for high school graduation.

---

[1] In the early primary grades, students are given cookies-and-milk breaks yet they are not required to brush their teeth afterwards. It is important to incorporate the concept of preventive care into the daily curriculum at this stage of a child's development. This can best be done by example.

[2] There should be a catalog of materials available for check-out privileges. For example, children's classics and other children's literature could be placed on tape for check-out. This would provide an opportunity for each student to listen to bedtime stories and therefore, to improve listening skills. Parents could be taught how to use such materials and how to participate in such home activities. Similar techniques and materials could be used for teaching fundamental math skills.

Parental Assistance

Often we hear that the children of the inner city do not have the appropriate home environment to induce good study habits; they lack books, magazines, adequate space to study, home assistance, and parental involvement. The Institute should develop a program that would permit parents to register their children in a home-based head-start program two years prior to entrance in kindergarten. The Institute would provide on-going training and supervision courses to assist parents in carrying out a head-start program for their children in their own homes. For example, part of the program could be organized to assist parents in helping their children develop listening skills. The Institute might provide parents with short stories to be read to their children, and supervisory techniques as to how they should be read. Some stories could be recorded on tape for children's listening. Parents would be instructed on how to generate discussions about the stories with their children. These techniques might be used with other preschool materials in similar parental-supervisory training programs.

Although there are many different types of roles played by parents, the following example further illustrates the possibility of maintaining a home-based head-start developmental program. Suppose we were concerned about how working parents can fit into such a program. The Institute could run neighborhood workshops to foster awareness of developmental growth, and provide working sessions for baby sitters to familiarize them with the creation and use of learning materials. Mobiles could be used in neighborhoods in which many homes are not conducive to a home-visit program.

Many working parents will find it difficult to participate in such a program because of the long work day. Therefore, the workshops must be short and well structured in order to facilitate their participation. A parent should not be expected to participate in a workshop more than once a week.

In the case of the parent who normally remains at home, the parent and child would be expected to participate in the workshops together. Workshops should be run at the Institute for parents who have transportation. Those parents who cannot travel would have to take advantage of the mobile and home-visit services.

Community Programs

Through the Institute, community programs can be organized to provide evening halfway houses (halfway between the school and the family) to provide an environment conducive to studying and learning. It is too expensive and presumptuous to think that halfway houses can be established to accommodate every urban student; they should focus on children ranging from four to eleven years of age and be equipped to accommodate 125 to 150 students. They should be well furnished, with adequate library facilities, lounging areas, kitchen facilities, and well lit parking areas. Activities should include general discussion groups, closed-circuit television programs and group and individual tutoring.[3]

How should halfway houses be staffed? How can they be financed? Obviously each house would have to be supervised by a professional, but the staff should be comprised of volunteers. The Institute for Urban Education and Human Resource Development would provide a training program for parents and other interested citizens who wished to participate in the program. Use of the house should be restricted to those students with one or more parents or guardians enrolled in the program. The program would be structured so as to prepare the participants for district certification as paraprofessionals in the areas for which they were trained. Those who enrolled in the training program would sign a voucher committing themselves to work in a halfway house for a specified amount of time. Depending upon the number of enrollees, the committed time could range from one to four hours per week for as long as one's child used the house.

A senior citizen volunteer program should be developed to enable senior citizens to assist the Institute with its home-visit program. They could also assist on the mobiles and in the halfway houses.

Likewise, there are many bright high school students who would be willing to work in evening programs: on mobiles, in halfway houses, and on home visits and security details. Admittedly, funds would have to be secured to pay the students. However, corporations and foundations, particularly in the urban districts, should be encouraged to assist the Institute in raising funds. Some students could nonetheless volunteer one evening a week to a "Big Brother/Big Sister" program designed and publicized to improve overall language, mathematics, and social skills of the urban youth in their community.

Social workers and welfare agencies should be encouraged to participate in the development and maintenance of all school-community programs, such as the halfway houses, and home-based head-start programs.

---

[3] Recently while I was aboard a flight a passenger had an asthma attack. The airline steward gave the victim oxygen, but the attack worsened. When I realized what was happening, I told the steward to cease using the oxygen and asked him to find some hot towels. After breathing in the hot steam for a few minutes, the passenger's asthma abated. The irony is that not one of the 200 passengers and crew knew how to use a simple first-aid technique that everyone should know by the time they reach their teens.

The Institute must provide a program for youth who have dropped out of school but would like to make a serious attempt to return, and for those who have acquired a high school diploma but realize that they have not received an appropriate education and seriously desire to return to the classroom.

Staff scheduling would be organized and monitored by the Institute, which would have the responsibility to seek and maintain funds for the houses. The sources of these funds might include the federal, state, and local governments, local industries and businesses, and foundations.

These are just a few of the many concerns that could be addressed through the Institute. Certainly it should address itself to the issues and recommendations outlined in the previous chapters.

The proposed Institute provides a structure to involve the entire urban community in the resolution of its educational and human resource problems. If the mayor, city council, school district officials, local industries and businesses, other elected officials, parents, students, and other citizens combine their energies and resources in a systematic way, the entire urban community can become a living curriculum.

Teacher Training and Tenure

Following the school of thought that the primary years are the most important, a student's educational development could be doomed if he or she were exposed to two incompetent teachers during the first four or five years of schooling.

Teacher competence has always been an unresolved issue in urban school districts. Any urban school administrator from the central office will contend that it is very difficult to acquire "competent" teachers who are willing to teach in the inner city. There are also problems of daily teacher absences and the enormous cost of merely filling each classroom with a teacher—whether or not the teacher is competent. Large urban school districts spend millions of dollars annually for substitute teachers.

Given the financial strains facing urban school districts, are there any alternatives to consider? The following are some questions regarding teacher competence that may be helpful in our quest to find alternative solutions: Should a national examination be given to all public school teachers to determine their competence in subject matter? Should those who fail be given a specified amount of time to re-educate themselves in order to maintain their teachers' licenses? Should urban school districts require a specified number of training sessions for all new teachers during their probationary period prior to tenure? Should teachers with tenure be required periodically to attend comprehensive in-service training sessions?

Should elementary teacher certification give license to teach all elementary grades? Should secondary certification apply to grade seven through grade twelve? Should there be a minimum competency test for teachers? The same types of questions also apply to school administrators.

In 1978, over five hundred Dallas public school teachers were administered a test of basic academic skills. One-third of those teachers did worse than the average high school junior in both English and mathematics. At least thirteen other states require their teachers to take a written examination for certification, and many other states are now considering examinations of this kind. It was reported in the *New York Times* that the American College Testing Program and other large college admission tests released data showing that of the nineteen major fields of study reported for freshmen in 1975, education majors ranked fourteenth on the English test and seventeenth in mathematics competency.[4]

After introducing a student-teacher competency test bill, Senator Hugh Fowler of Colorado spoke at a conference for state elementary school principals and expressed his concerns about a teachers' association in one of the larger cities in Colorado which initiated a teacher letter-writing campaign in opposition to his competency test bill. Senator Fowler offered to show his collection of letters to anyone who doubted the need for a teacher competency test. He felt that the letters graphically illustrated the teachers' writing and spelling deficiencies.[5] Likewise, the governor of Arkansas has signed into law a bill that requires the state board of education to formulate new regulations and procedures for teacher certification that include competency testing.

Teacher competence is essential in the cognitive and affective aspects of the teaching process. This is especially true in the primary and elementary grades. We have done well in developing instruments that test the cognitive strength of teachers, but we have no appropriate instruments to effectively measure the affective behavior and characteristics of teachers in the classroom.

Consequently, the following recommendations should be strongly considered by the urban school board of trustees:

1. It is recommended that no teacher who is trained for teaching the primary grades be assigned to the intermediate grades without appropriate preparation. Often teachers move up and down through the elementary grades with no special training preceding such a move. If an instructor is

---

[4] "Report on Inadequate Teachers," *New York Times*, 18 September 1979, sec. C, p. 1.
[5] *Legislative Review* 9 (19 February 1979): 1.

teaching a second- or third-grade class, he or she should receive some kind of training before being assigned to a fourth– or fifth–grade class. If the school district is unable to financially provide in-service training to accommodate the teacher's needs, the teacher may have to return to school for additional training.

2. It is recommended that a teacher who has been certified to teach grades one through three be given a two-year internship at each grade level. After each of the two-year internships an evaluation of the teacher's performance should be made. Following the sixth year, through collaborations with his or her supervisors and the principal, the teacher should be placed at the grade level most applicable to his or her style of teaching, personality, knowledge of the subject matter, and teaching capabilities. Grade level placement should be based upon these evaluations. Tenure should be considered only if the teacher has demonstrated a) the ability to teach, b) professional growth in his or her area of specialization and, c) has completed the Master of Arts degree for the primary grades.

3. It is recommended that once the teacher is placed at the appropriate grade level he or she not be abandoned. A program should be effected to encourage continuous self-growth, training for other levels of teaching, and the acceptance of other responsibilities within the community-school system.

4. It is recommended that the criteria outlined with regard to the teaching of grades one through three be extended to include grades four through six, seven through nine, and ten through twelve.

5. It is recommended that urban school districts seek financial assistance from state and federal governments to institute a developmental program for the purpose of effecting an environment to measure the affective behavior and characteristics of teachers. This type of affective center could be programmed through the Institute.

6. It is recommended that each state develop a teachers' minimum competency test that is required of all instructors, and that those teachers who are identified as undertrained and/or scholastically disadvantaged be given a specified amount of time in which to remove their deficiencies. There will always be financial crises surrounding urban education. Since the above-mentioned training would not cost more than would one to three graduate courses, each teacher or his or her professional union should be expected to finance the cost, and this cost should be viewed as part of the expense of his or her ongoing professional training and development. This should be required throughout the teacher's career. The cost of this type of professional training is tax deductible.

Desegregation

There may not be any need for more research on the need for and importance of desegregation. But there is a need for some alternative to busing, especially in those urban school districts in which seventy percent or more of the students are Black. The following recommendations are offered to accompany existing desegregation programs:

1. It is recommended that school districts include in their desegregation plans a teacher and administrator distribution program, and that members of both groups be rotated to different schools within the district every three to five years to insure that a balance of race is maintained in all schools.[6] There are a number of significant reasons for such a plan. One of the arguments against busing white students into a black district is the lack of qualified teachers. A distribution plan would invalidate this argument and expand teachers' and administrators' sensitivity to the diverse student and faculty populations. The rotating system would more equitably distribute the qualified teachers and administrators and prevent any one school from bearing a disproportionate share of less competent or under-trained teachers. Finally, it would make it less difficult to identify and eliminate incompetence within the system.

2. It is recommended that the distribution program apply to all staff personnel, including supervisors, custodians, and clerical workers.

3. Sports activities have probably been successful in breaking more new ground in race relations than any other factor. Because of this success, the following recommendations are offered:

a. City-wide teams should be organized to replace the school team program. This would minimize separation and segregation in sports activities in which whites are pulling for a white victory and Blacks for a black victory. It would introduce a community-wide spirit and camaraderie rather than a "them-and-us" perception of competition.

b. The development of city-wide teams should be achieved through tryouts. Depending upon the size of the school district, the number of teams might vary from six to ten. Larger cities would have more teams.

---

[6] In order to maintain continuity, principals should be permitted to see a beginning class through graduation. For example, if a principal is assigned to a K-3 school, she or he should be permitted to remain with the school for four years. This will allow the principal to see an entering kindergarten class through its graduation at the end of the third grade. The principal should then be transferred to another school. This should apply to 4-6, 7-9 and 10-12. The distribution plan should be staggered to insure continuity. That is, no school should lose more than one-third of its administrative staff or teachers in any one year.

c. The number of leagues should depend upon the number of teams. If there is more than one league, a playoff series would be required at the end of the season to determine the city-wide champion. The selection process could easily be computerized to insure that each team be of a competitive caliber.

d. Each school should provide a comprehensive intramural program of sports activities for those students who choose not to or who cannot make the city-wide teams.

e. This type of program should not eliminate the teams in the city-wide league from outside competition. In fact, all the teams should have some outside exposure. Neither should those who participate in such a system be banned from competing in state-wide tournaments. The only difference is that the school system, rather than a particular school, would be represented in the state-wide competition. Thus, the school district's city-wide champions would be the representatives in the state-wide tournaments. This system should certainly have a positive effect upon race relations in the urban community. It might very well reduce the violence that is threatening competitive sports in urban areas because of local team rivalry and peer identity.

Alternative Testing

Discussions continue between testing specialists and Black, Chicano, Puerto Rican, and other minority educators regarding the issue of test bias against minorities and the related issue of college admission. What is striking about these discussions is that minority educators and test specialists are still putting forth the same arguments they used four or five years ago.

Nowadays the emphasis is on minimum competency testing. Arthur Wise claims that "a minority of students are not learning and a minority of teachers are not teaching. There is little reason to think that minimum competency testing will solve that."[7] Minimum competency testing is a new process based upon traditional testing phenomena, and it is absurd and unfair to the student to expect that this process will get to the root of the achievement problem.

Minority teachers, counselors, college admission officers, and educational administrators insist that present-day testing practices discriminate against all minority students, but most especially against those who are

---

[7] Arthur Wise, "Why Minimum Competency Testing Will Not Improve Education," *Educational Leadership* 36 (May 1979): 546.

disadvantaged by an increasing retardation of the educational and environmental conditions in which they are expected to develop and learn. However, testing specialists persist in their view that aptitude tests are as valid for predicting present and later performance of minority students as they are for majority students. What they have implied, in more blunt language, is that minority students do not perform as well on tests of academic competency as do advantaged white Anglo-Saxon students, and that minority students' actual academic performance is, therefore, very likely to be lower than that of their advantaged white Anglo-Saxon counterparts.

Several reasons account for the current failure to resolve the arguments about minority student test bias, but principal among them is that minority educators and testing specialists are not discussing the same issues. Minorities are concerned about the effects of testing on minority students; they charge that tests inhibit minority students from moving freely through the educational system into postsecondary educational institutions and thence into upper-level professional careers. On the other hand, members of the testing community have concerned themselves with a different issue, that of the predictive validity of tests applied to various ethnic groups; the more important issue—the effects of testing on social and economic ordering—has been ignored.

Blacks and other minorities are not concerned about predictive validity. What they are concerned about is the fact that tests serve as discriminatory devices when they are used in any type of placement, particularly in college admission. This concern, along with the concern about the use of national standardized test scores to virtually irrevocably determine a student's educational track, adequately define the issues facing minorities with regard to test bias.

The minority-group concern about the effects of testing encompasses the elementary and secondary grade levels as well. However, the possible damage is much greater. Tests are administered by teachers who have little or no background in testing. Likewise, administrators who have little or no testing background have the responsibility for making decisions about test usage. In the final analysis, the already disadvantaged child is further disadvantaged through such odious methods as tracking, which is based upon standardized test scores. Thus, ghetto and other disadvantaged children find themselves automatically tracked into "slow" classes. This marks the beginning of ten to twelve years of debilitation inflicted upon the inner-city student and is enough to insure his underdevelopment and his unacceptability as a college entrant.

This is not to imply that testing should be banned. On the contrary, it is recognized that while the testing phenomenon has increased racial polarization in our society, it has also advanced technological growth fifty years beyond the average human's understanding. Just as the testing phenomenon has been used in the past to prevent positive social change for Blacks and other minorities, it can be used to increase opportunities for those same disadvantaged groups. This can be done by developing alternative tests to be used as an integral part of the teacher's instruction rather than as a measure of the student's achievement or ability.

Language Skills Testing. The assessment of minority student language skills has emerged as a serious and unresolved problem for college and university directors of developmental programs for minority students. They are faced with the problem of the increasing number of students who enter college with an inadequate educational background. In most cases these inadequacies are identified as essential skill deficiencies in language communication.

The primary objective of directors of supportive services programs is to bring minority students from their skill level at the time of their admission to college to the skill level required for college-level work. However, the existing college admission testing programs do not meet the needs of the directors for several reasons. Typically, low scores earned by minority students on admission tests identify them as weak in verbal and/or mathematical aptitude and academic achievement. This identification is helpful, but test scores like those used in the College Board or American College Testing batteries do not identify the specific basic skills or subject matter in which their weakness lies.

Recently, the Scholastic Aptitude Test was altered. It now has three components. Thirty minutes were cut from the two original tests, fifteen each from the verbal and mathematical components, and a thirty-minute test of standard written English was added. The purpose of the new test arrangement was to provide more information about students' English usage to the college admission officers, English departments, and directors of supportive services. However, when I surveyed twenty colleges and universities in the Philadelphia area, I found that only one English department was aware of the new component, and the chairman claimed that the department was staffed to teach literature, not English grammar.

Only a few of the directors of supportive services questioned were aware of the new test, and none of them had taken the test seriously enough to investigate its validity or harm factors. However, admission officers were using the scores from the new test as part of the over-all criteria for student selection.

Too often this is the case. Tests are developed without the input of those who will or should be using them. In general, this leads to the improper use of tests; the essential prescriptions that should be developed for each item and accompany the test never advance beyond the developmental stage. The responsibility becomes that of the teachers, most of whom have not received appropriate training in this area.

The State of New York requires that the test results of national testing firms be published and shared with school district personnel. The testing firms are lobbying this issue in Washington, trying to abort what might become a national trend.

The secrecy or publication of the test results will not get to the root of the problem. The testing process must become more localized in order to properly treat the academic problems of a particular school district. School districts should be working with the national testing firms to develop tests designed to detect and measure the particular problems of their students. But test development should not be done in a vacuum. Diagnosis and prescription must be done simultaneously.

Linguistic specialists and English teachers agree that there is a great need for alternative tests and accompanying materials to facilitate the teaching of classroom English. This plea for alternative tests is not made simply because minority groups seem to do worse on standardized tests than do advantaged white Anglo-Saxon students. The problem is more serious. Alternative tests are necessary because present standardized examinations do not adequately measure the linguistic elements that interfere with minority students' achievement in American classroom English.

Only recently have real issues gained recognition surrounding the linguistic problems faced by minority students in learning to communicate in standard classroom English. Complex issues are now well documented in various publications, focusing on black English vernacular and related black biculturalism, as well as their relevance to academic achievement within the medium of standard American English.[8]

Labov, in a conference entitled *Language in Education for Minorities,* claimed that among the major studies of black English vernacular there exists a remarkably uniform grammar, comparatively free of regional differences and used by both youth on the streets and adults at home. Labov said that in many ways the grammar of the black vernacular is closely aligned with that of classroom English grammar, and that "many of its marked features are general characteristics of regional Southern syntax . . . but extended and generalized to a point far beyond the forms found in most non-standard dialect . . . this same vernacular preserves many grammatical features which clearly reflect a Creole background: the habitual invariant *be* of *He always be doing that*; the remote present perfect *been* as in *I been own one of those.*" He further stated that there is a

---

[8] *See* Dillard, Labov, and Torrey.

need for alternative tests in order to better isolate these "marked features," and that the test information will facilitate the development of language instruction.[9] Conclusions of the studies heretofore mentioned indicate that there does indeed exist a black English dialect and that it must be considered in the teaching of the standard English dialect to black students.

If black English exists as a dialect or language apart from standard English, with grammar, composition, intonation, and meanings that are clearly different from those of standard English, then the objective of English language instruction for black students should be the recognition of those components of standard English that differ significantly from their dialect. Otherwise, Blacks may misunderstand standard English phrasing that sounds very much like black vernacular phrasing but differs sharply in meaning.

Biculturalism and bilingualism are studied by psychologists and specialists in linguistics as factors contributing to cultural and cognitive confusion in the treatment of academic material.[10] The language patterns of Chicano and Puerto Rican students in particular have not received adequate attention from specialists in psychology and linguistics, particularly as those patterns relate to the academic achievement of those students in institutions of higher education.[11] Both language and culture need intensive study for purposes of academic assessment and treatment.

Studies of the language of Spanish-speaking minority groups in this country are not as advanced as black language studies, but important work has appeared during the last few years. Some sociolinguistic features of the English and Spanish used by Puerto Ricans in New York City are reported in the extensive work on bilingualism carried out by Fishman, Cooper, Ma and Herasimchuk.[12] So far, very few scholarly studies have been directed to the educational consequences of Spanish-English bilingualism for older, college-age students, although it is recognized as a serious problem.

[9] William Labov, Professor of Linguistics at the University of Pennsylvania, indicated that some of the language problems associated with minority students were first raised in the 1964 conference on Social Dialects and Language Learning (Shuy, 1964), and in early meetings of "Project Literacy," a consortium of research groups focusing on reading (Leven & Williams, 1970); and later in New York City (Labov, Cohen, Robins, and Lewis, 1968); Detroit (Wolfram, 1969); Hillsboro, North Carolina (Anshen, 1969); Washington (Fasold, 1971); Los Angeles (Legum et al., 1971); Berkeley (Mitchell, Kernon, 1969); and Buffalo, New York (Fickett, 1970).

[10] William F. Mackey, "The Description of Bilingualism," *Canadian Journal of Linguistics,* Vol. VII, No. 2 (1962).

[11] Jack Ornstein, *Study of Minority Students' Treatment of Standard English as a Function of Dialect or Bilingual Background,* Conference at Educational Testing Services (Princeton, N.J., 1974).

[12] Joshua Fishman, Robert L. Cooper, Roxanna Ma, and others, *Bilingualism in the Barrio,* Final Report on OECD-1-7-062817 (Washington, D.C.: Office of Education, 1968).

Assuming that verbal facility is a universal human skill appearing in all language groups and developed most highly in one's native tongue, it might behoove educators to begin identifying and measuring those verbal skills against standard classroom English. One way to meet the challenge is for minority educators to assume leadership in the development of alternative tests, academic assessment projects, and related research projects on testing directed toward minority students in elementary and secondary schools. Such examinations would assist teachers in diagnosing areas of specific language weakness in students' use of classroom English; from such diagnoses educators could formulate appropriate perscriptions for instruction. Eventually, a series of tests tailored to the specific needs of each identifiably disadvantaged minority group could be developed.

There is, of course, a difference in the approach used to bring classroom English to Blacks and that used in teaching Chicanos, Puerto Ricans and other non-English speaking students. For example, the teacher assumes that the native language of a Chicano or Puerto Rican is Spanish. Therefore, English is taught as a second language to these students. Because teachers assume that black students speak English, it is not taught as a second language to them. Although English should be taught as a second language to Chicanos and Puerto Ricans, it is erroneous to assume that they all know how to speak Spanish. Most of them do not speak Spanish correctly. Much of their speech patterns include a mixture of broken Spanish and broken English. Likewise, many black students speak an English dialect sufficiently different from classroom English to require English to be taught as a second language to them.

The fact remains that there has been little research on the standard English competency of minority students entering colleges and universities because minority enrollment has been low and the linguistic issues are complex. Nor have there been sufficient minority staff members in colleges and universities capable of assuming research leadership for the completion of project components requiring insight and understanding not likely to be possessed by traditional research specialists. Such research is important for the instruction and guidance of college-bound minority students and for those already attending college.

Mathematics Skills Testing. There remains much to be desired, too, regarding the testing process measuring students' performance in mathematics. We have been effective in measuring whether a student has mastered a skill or a particular area of content in mathematics. But we have failed miserably in our efforts to identify the student's exact deficiencies and use the testing process to aid us in teaching.

During the past decade, educators have focused their attention on the improvement of reading skills to the detriment of students' mathematical competency. Consequently, it should not be surprising to us to be told that students' achievement in mathematics is dropping, particularly in the urban schools.

A student's performance in mathematics need not depend upon reading competency. This correlation is the consequence of our educational philosophy. We are a reading society, and we have made our students reading dependent. Hence, they get very little opportunity to develop the mental skills necessary to achieve in mathematics.

To make a student dependent upon any one mode of instruction is to take away that student's opportunity to apply his or her own cognitive style to a set of instructions. Book dependency serves as an example of this. The proposition that a child who cannot read cannot learn basic mathematics results in a further disadvantage. Teachers, nonetheless, tend to make the student book dependent during the early years of his or her elementary school development. Consequently, a student who experiences reading difficulties will experience equal difficulties in achieving in mathematics.

Likewise, testing plays an important role in the teaching of arithmetic. We can do an excellent job in measuring a student's achievement in arithmetic, but we have not developed efficient instruments to identify, or isolate, the exact difficulty that is preventing the student from mastering a particular skill or an area of mathematical content. Consequently, achievement tests separate students into two categories: those who have achieved and those who have not.

Standardized diagnostic tests attempt to identify a student's difficulties. However, even the best tests available are not descriptive enough. The data from such tests do not reveal to the teacher exactly what the student has not learned. In fact, we should be equally concerned about what the student has not mastered and what the student has learned incorrectly.

Most of the testing that takes place in the classroom is done with teacher-made tests. If very few teachers have adequate training in developing test items, then it is reasonable to assume that much of such testing works against the student.

Since the testing process is essential to the teaching of mathematics, it is imperative that we refine it as much as possible. Elementary school students are in the process of building cognitive skills for learning and understanding mathematics. It is therefore especially important that elementary school teachers attain a mastery of the testing process and understand fully how to incorporate it into their teaching. Teachers must know as early as possible where the student is experiencing difficulty in his or her development and mastery of a particular skill. Only through efficient and effective testing can we maximize our capability in identifying students' deficiencies.

The following process should be considered by those who are responsible for the district mathematics curriculum. It consists of three fundamental stages: prognosis, diagnosis, and prescriptions.

Prognosis: A teacher must establish a set of expected outcomes—what should the student learn and at what level of proficiency? In many school districts the teacher is not fully aware of the prerequisite skills associated with each expected outcome. It is imperative that the school district organize a skill continuum for primary and intermediate school teachers. However, it must be translated into a curriculum for classroom use. The entire continuum should be correlated with the content of the textbooks and materials adopted. Teachers should fully understand the relationship between each skill in the continuum and the corresponding content in the texts.

Unless the teacher is fully cognizant of what is expected of his or her students, it is impossible to perform an appropriate prognosis.

Diagnosis: The teacher must diagnostically determine the cognitive skills of each student in terms of that student's proficiencies and deficiencies. It is not enough to administer a test to measure the student's achievement or mastery of certain skills; the teacher must also determine the student's deficiencies or lack of skill development for the levels defined in the prognosis.

In order for teachers to maximize their effectiveness in diagnosing students' deficiencies and strengths, they must be trained to develop their own diagnostic instruments.

However, diagnosing cognitive skills is not sufficient for developing instruction. A thorough diagnosis also includes the affective aspects of the student. One way this may be achieved is by identifying the students' interests as well as their weaknesses and strengths. Likewise, not all children are disadvantaged in the same manner; some are socially or economically disadvantaged, others are educationally disadvantaged, and still others are disadvantaged in more than one way. It is necessary for teachers to find out as much as possible about their students' disadvantages, interests, and concerns.

Only when the teacher has thoroughly defined the expected outcomes and has thoroughly diagnosed students' interests, strengths, and weaknesses does the teacher have the appropriate cognitive and affective knowledge to design a specific method of instruction.

Prescription: Prescriptive instruction should be developed only after a thorough evaluation of the data gained from the diagnostic instruments. Teacher input and full understanding of the processes advancing from diagnosis to prescription are fundamental to the development of appropriate prescriptive instruction as well. For example, if we had two sets of students, one from a large urban apartment complex and another from a suburban area, should the teacher use the same prescription and teaching techniques to teach the two groups the concept of magnitude? If a group of students were from home environments in which their financial resources barely meet the exigencies of survival, should a traditional course in business mathematics be taught to them and, if so, when?

Although the exact reasons why languages and mathematics present fundamental problems to minority students are debatable, it is nonetheless clear that past testing practices have not worked to the advantage of the urban student. It is also evident that this disadvantage cannot be overcome without the development of alternative tests which are more descriptive in design.

References

Chomsky, N. *Aspects of The Theory of Syntax.* Cambridge, Mass.: MIT Press, 1965.

DeStefano, Johanna S. *Language, Society, and Education: A Profile of Black English.* Worthington, Ohio: Charles A. Jones, 1973.

Dillard, J. L. *Black English.* New York: Random House, 1972.

Fishman, Joshua; Cooper, Robert L.; Ma, Roxanna, and others. *Bilingualism in the Barrio.* Final Report on OECD-1-7-062817. Washington, D.C.: Office of Education, 1968.

Labov, William; Cohen, Paul; Robins, Clarence; and Lewis, John. *A Study of the Nonstandard English of Negro and Puerto Rican Speakers in New York City.* Cooperative Research Report 3288. Philadelphia: U.S. Regional Survey, 1972.

Mackey, William F. "The Description of Bilingualism." *Canadian Journal of Linguistics,* Vol. VII, No. 2, 1962.

Mitchell-Kernan, Claudia. *Language Behavior in a Black Urban Community.* Language-Behavior Research Laboratory Working Paper No. 23. Berkeley: Language-Behavior Research Laboratory, 1969.

Ornstein, Jack. *Study of Minority Students' Treatment of Standard English as a Function of Dialect or Bilingual Background.* Conference at Educational Testing Services. Princeton, New Jersey, 1974.

Shuy, Roger, ed. *Social Dialects and Language Learning.* Champaign, Ill.: National Conference of Teachers of English, 1964.

Torrey, Jane W. *The Language of Black Children in the Early Grades.* Monograph, Connecticut College, 1972.

Wise, Arthur. "Why Minimum Competency Testing Will Not Improve Education." *Educational Leadership* 36 (May 1979): 546.

Index

About the Authors

JAMES E. ANDERSON, Associate Professor of Curriculum and Instruction, University of Houston, Houston, Texas

H. PRENTICE BAPTISTE, JR., Associate Professor of Curriculum and Instruction, University of Houston, Houston, Texas

MATTIE R. CROSSLEY, Instructional Consultant, Memphis City Schools, Memphis, Tennessee

MARK GELLERSON, Assistant Professor of Economics, Southern Illinois University, Carbondale, Illinois

CLEMENT B. G. LONDON, Associate Professor of Education, Fordham University at Lincoln Center, New York, New York

CLAUDE MAYBERRY, JR., Associate Provost and Special Assistant to the President, Lecturer in Mathematics, Colgate University, Hamilton, New York

WILLIAM H. SWEET, Principal, Riverview Junior High School, Memphis, Tennessee

ASCD Publications, Fall 1980

Yearbooks

Considered Action for Curriculum Improvement
(610-80186) $9.75
Education for an Open Society
(610-74012) $8.00
Evaluation as Feedback and Guide
(610-17700) $6.50
Feeling, Valuing, and the Art of Growing:
Insights into the Affective
(610-77104) $9.75
Life Skills in School and Society
(610-17786) $5.50
Lifelong Learning—A Human Agenda
(610-79160) $9.75
A New Look at Progressive Education
(610-17812) $8.00
Perspectives on Curriculum Development
1776-1976 (610-76078) $9.50
Schools in Search of Meaning
(610-75044) $8.50
Perceiving, Behaving, Becoming: A New Focus
for Education (610-17278) $5.00

Books and Booklets

About Learning Materials (611-78134) $4.50
Action Learning: Student Community Service
Projects (611-74018) $2.50
Adventuring, Mastering, Associating: New
Strategies for Teaching Children
(611-76080) $5.00
Approaches to Individualized Education
(611-80204) $4.75
Bilingual Education for Latinos
(611-78142) $6.75
Classroom-Relevant Research in the Language
Arts (611-78140) $7.50
Clinical Supervision—A State of the Art Review
(611-80194) $3.75
Curricular Concerns in a Revolutionary Era
(611-17852) $6.00
Curriculum Leaders: Improving Their Influence
(611-76084) $4.00
Curriculum Materials 1980 (611-80198) $3.00
Curriculum Theory (611-77112) $7.00
Degrading the Grading Myths: A Primer of
Alternatives to Grades and Marks
(611-76082) $6.00
Educating English-Speaking Hispanics
(611-80202) $6.50
Elementary School Mathematics: A Guide to
Current Research (611-75056) $5.00
Eliminating Ethnic Bias in Instructional
Materials: Comment and Bibliography
(611-74020) $3.25
Global Studies: Problems and Promises for
Elementary Teachers (611-76086) $4.50
Handbook of Basic Citizenship Competencies
(611-80196) $4.75
Humanistic Education: Objectives and
Assessment (611-78136) $4.75
Learning More About Learning
(611-17310) $2.00
Middle School in the Making
(611-74024) $5.00

The Middle School We Need
(611-75060) $2.50
Moving Toward Self-Directed Learning
(611-79166) $4.75
Multicultural Education: Commitments, Issues,
and Applications (611-77108) $7.00
Needs Assessment: A Focus for Curriculum
Development (611-75048) $4.00
Observational Methods in the Classroom
(611-17948) $3.50
Open Education: Critique and Assessment
(611-75054) $4.75
Partners: Parents and Schools
(611-79168) $4.75
Professional Supervision for Professional
Teachers (611-75046) $4.50
Reschooling Society: A Conceptual Model
(611-17950) $2.00
The School of the Future—NOW
(611-17920) $3.75
Schools Become Accountable: A PACT
Approach (611-74016) $3.50
The School's Role as Moral Authority
(611-77110) $4.50
Selecting Learning Experiences: Linking
Theory and Practice (611-78138) $4.75
Social Studies for the Evolving Individual
(611-17952) $3.00
Staff Development: Staff Liberation
(611-77106) $6.50
Supervision: Emerging Profession
(611-17796) $5.00
Supervision in a New Key (611-17926) $2.50
Urban Education: The City as a Living
Curriculum (611-80206) $6.50
What Are the Sources of the Curriculum?
(611-17522) $1.50
Vitalizing the High School (611-74026) $3.50
Developmental Characteristics of Children and
Youth (wall chart) (611-75058) $2.00

Discounts on quantity orders of same title to
single address: 10-49 copies, 10%; 50 or more
copies, 15%. Make checks or money orders
payable to ASCD. Orders totaling $20.00 or
less must be prepaid. Orders from institutions
and businesses must be on official purchase
order form. Shipping and handling charges will
be added to billed purchase orders. *Please be
sure to list the stock number of each publication, shown in parentheses.*

Subscription to *Educational Leadership*—$18.00
a year. ASCD Membership dues: Regular (subscription [$18] and yearbook)—$34.00 a year;
Comprehensive (includes subscription [$18]
and yearbook plus other books and booklets
distributed during period of membership)—
$44.00 a year.

Order from:

**Association for Supervision and
Curriculum Development
225 North Washington Street
Alexandria, Virginia 22314**